Profession and Purpose

PROFESSION
A Resource Guide for MBA Careers in Sustainability
AND PURPOSE

Katie Kross

Greenleaf
PUBLISHING

© 2009 Greenleaf Publishing Limited

Published by Greenleaf Publishing Limited
Aizlewood's Mill
Nursery Street
Sheffield S3 8GG
UK
www.greenleaf-publishing.com

Printed in Great Britain by MPG Biddles Limited

Mixed Sources
Product group from well-managed
forests and other controlled sources
www.fsc.org Cert no. SA-COC-1565
© 1996 Forest Stewardship Council

Cover by LaliAbril.com

British Library Cataloguing in Publication Data:

Kross, Katie.
  Profession and purpose : a resource guide for MBA careers
  in sustainability.
  1. Social responsibility of business. 2. Green marketing--
  Vocational guidance. 3. Sustainable development--
  Vocational guidance.
  I. Title
  658.4'083'023-dc22

ISBN-13: 9781906093297

Contents

Preface

Over the past several years of working with MBA students at both Duke University's Fuqua School of Business and the University of North Carolina's Kenan-Flagler Business School, I have come to realize that the career paths that fall under the broad umbrella of "sustainability" are as diverse as the students themselves. One student may come in to talk to me about social entrepreneurship in West Africa, and the next will be seeking advice about cleantech venture capital careers in Silicon Valley; a third will be interested in greening global supply chains. Corporate social responsibility, sustainable product marketing, microfinance, green real estate development, renewable energy, and other interests all likewise fall under the sustainability umbrella at times.

Because of this diversity, it is often hard for career management centers at business schools to address sustainability-related career options in a comprehensive way. Many sustainability-related companies and nonprofits are not accustomed to on-campus recruiting. Others have not historically hired MBAs at all. MBA students and alumni interested in sustainability careers are often left to navigate their own internship and job search paths.

That's where this guide comes in. Whether you are focused on an off-campus search or participating in the on-campus recruiting process, there are sustainability-specific career resources you should know about. You'll need to be well versed in sustainability news and trends, and network at the right events, conferences, and company presentations. You also need to know about industry- and discipline-specific websites that post sustainability jobs for positions with titles like Corporate Social Responsibility Manager, Socially Responsible Investing Analyst, and Renewable Energy Market Analyst.

Through hundreds of conversations with MBA students, professionals, and recruiters, as well as my own personal experience, I have compiled some of the most helpful job search resources for MBAs interested in sustainability careers. This book will give you ideas for researching companies, making the most of your networking, identifying job and internship openings, and preparing for interviews.

This guide will not answer all of your questions about careers that incorporate social and environmental considerations. The topics are too many and the field is ever-evolving. Nor will it tell you definitively which career you are best suited for. There are other books devoted to helping you assess your personal goals, expectations, and job fit (some of which I reference in "Recommended reading" on page 141).

Rather, this guide is intended to compile in one place the helpful resources, websites, key terms, and job search tips for many of the possible career paths for an MBA interested in sustainability. No matter what stage of your MBA career search process you're in, this guide will help you better understand your career options in the many fields of sustainability, and direct you to resources and job search strategies.

About the author

Katie Kross is a sustainability career coach, MBA student advisor, and business school administrator. She has directed sustainability programs for the Corporate Sustainability Initiative at Duke University and the Center for Sustainable Enterprise at the University of North Carolina's Kenan-Flagler Business School. An MBA graduate herself, she has developed career support and mentoring programs for students interested in sustainability and counseled hundreds of individual students and alumni on their career paths. She has also served on the boards of the US Partnership for Education for Sustainable Development and the Triangle, North Carolina professional chapter of Net Impact.

Acknowledgments

A million thanks go to the following individuals who contributed insights and research to this guide:

- Allison Adams
- Coleman Bigelow
- Kelly Boone
- Jay Carlis
- David Carlson
- Michelle Chislett
- Jeff Gowdy
- Shawn Graham
- Marc Heisterkamp
- Mark Hilpert
- Lindsay James
- Lisa Jones Christensen
- Natacha Kiler
- Annie Lux
- Marcy Scott Lynn
- Marc Major
- Jeff Mittelstadt
- Sitar Mody
- Matt Nash
- Katherine Neebe
- Deb Parsons
- Libby Reder
- Tim Scheu
- Graham Sinclair
- Val Smith
- Rebecca Swartz
- Jessica Thomas
- Ruth Tolman
- Tracy Triggs-Matthews
- Dan Vermeer
- Sam Walden
- Napoleon Wallace
- Ellen Weinreb
- Sheri Willoughby
- Brad Wood

My deepest gratitude also goes to my family and friends, and, most of all, Scott, for making it possible for me to pursue a sustainability career that I love.

Part I

Evaluating your options

Getting started:
MBA careers in sustainability

Everywhere you look these days, the words "sustainability," "green," and "corporate social responsibility" are flooding the business press. Companies in every industry are rushing to add climate change strategies, corporate citizenship reports, and green products. Entirely new disciplines in fields like sustainability consulting, carbon trading, and socially responsible investing are emerging. Wal-Mart, Toyota, GE, and other corporations are revolutionizing their industries by making sustainability not only a part of their own corporate strategy, but also a requirement for their supply chain partners.

In January 2007, *BusinessWeek*'s cover read, "Imagine a world in which socially responsible and eco-friendly practices actually boost a company's bottom line. It's closer than you think." By 2008, nearly 80% of the largest 250 companies worldwide were issuing corporate responsibility reports, up from about 50% in 2005.[1] Dell, Pepisco, Google, and other corporations had pledged to become carbon neutral. NBC Universal held an entire week of television programming with "green" themes. Brands like Starbucks, Gap, and Apple began appealing to conscientious young consumers with their Product(RED)™ campaign, devoting a portion of profits to development organizations in Africa. And manufacturers in every industry unveiled an impressive slate of new eco-friendly products ranging from energy-efficient televisions to biodegradable hotel room keys.

Sustainability holds the promise of an exciting new approach to business — one in which business goals are aligned with social and environmental goals, in which it *is* possible to "do well by doing good." And, while sustainability certainly will not cure all the world's ills, it is clear that a new era of business responsibility and green innovation is upon us. Multinational corporations are recognizing that we live in an increasingly resource-constrained world, and that more accountability for corporate social and environmental impacts will accrue to them. More importantly, forward-thinking executives understand that sustainability can present new opportunities for competitive advantage — whether that is by reducing costs, minimizing risk, appealing to increasingly conscientious customers, or reaching new markets entirely.

With the growth of this field comes a host of interesting new career opportunities for MBAs. As companies are grappling with challenges like how to develop social return on investment (SROI) metrics or understand the potential impact of corporate carbon footprints on stock prices, there are new opportunities for the next generation of managers — managers who are not only trained in traditional MBA fundamentals but also grounded in an understanding of the multifaceted social and environmental challenges facing 21st-century global business leaders. Entirely new career paths are opening up to MBAs interested in sustainability: sustainable venture capital, green marketing, corporate social responsibility management, carbon credit trading, and sustainability consulting, to name a few.

Perhaps even more than corporate executives, MBA students understand this trend. The next generation of managers can see that the future of business will require a new set of skills and responsibilities. Between 2003 and 2008, membership in Net Impact — the global organization for MBAs and business professionals interested in sustainability — increased more than four-

Conscientious MBAs

You are not alone. A recent study by David Montgomery of Stanford University and Catherine Ramus of UC Santa Barbara found that over 97% of MBAs surveyed would be willing to sacrifice salary to work for a company that was committed to social and environmental responsibility and ethics.

The researchers surveyed 759 MBAs at 11 top business schools, and found that, on average, the graduating MBAs said they would sacrifice 14% of their expected salary to work for a responsible company.[2]

fold. By March 2009, over 130 business schools had a Net Impact chapter. Around the world, MBA students realize that a different model will be required for businesses in the coming decades.

That's where you come in. You understand this. You want a career where you can use your business skills to affect society and the environment in a positive way. You understand that the social, environmental, and governance challenges facing business are only going to become more complex, rather than less. You know intuitively that there is not only a moral imperative but also a compelling business case for companies to manage their social and environmental impacts. You see sustainability as the way forward for business, and a path to strategic career opportunities for you.

But what exactly does that mean for your career? And how are you going to land your dream job? *Profession and Purpose* is a practical guide to help MBA students and alumni pursue sustainability-related careers. This guide compiles in one place tips and resources for MBA-level careers in a wide range of fields — corporate social responsibility, corporate environmental management, cleantech venture capital, green building, sustainability consulting, and others — and discusses specific job search strategies for each. It includes information about the types of roles and responsibilities candidates can expect in each of these fields, as well as example job titles, useful websites, recommended reading, and advice from recent MBA graduates about their job searches.

Sustainability careers span a wide range of social and environmental career options — from "green" product marketing to social entrepreneurship to climate change consulting. MBA students have to consider both the type of functional role they are interested in, and the size and type of organization. The guide will help you navigate the maze of sustainability-related MBA career options, and point you on a path to success.

Sustainability is a constantly evolving field and, as such, it is impossible to cover all the potential career options available to you. However, this guide is intended to be the most complete compilation of resources you can find on MBA careers in sustainability. In the following pages, you'll find not only specific job-hunting advice, but also inspiration. As the stories of MBAs profiled in this guide attest, there *are* careers for MBAs in sustainability. And there are exciting opportunities to integrate sustainability into your career, whether you are working for a big corporation or a startup company, an investment bank, or a social entrepreneur.

You really can change the world through your career. Start today.

What is sustainability?

Let's start with the basics: what does "sustainability" really mean? There are a host of buzzwords associated with this term and, across the board, it means different things to different companies and individuals. But, fundamentally, sustainability is the concept that organizations can approach social and environmental challenges as business opportunities. That is, by addressing social and environmental considerations, a company may not only minimize any negative social and environmental impacts of its business operations (along with associated costs and risks), but may also realize new sources of competitive advantage such as creating new product or supply chain innovations. As the Dow Jones Sustainability Index summarizes it:

> Corporate sustainability is a business approach that creates long-term shareholder value by embracing opportunities and managing risks deriving from economic, environmental and social developments.

Another often-referred-to definition is the "Brundtland Commission" definition: "sustainable development is development that meets the needs of the present without compromising the ability of future generations to meet their own needs."[3] While this definition is less specifically business-oriented than others, it is widely used in sustainability circles.

When it comes to business applications, the term "sustainability" is often used as a broad umbrella that encompasses a host of social and environmental impact issues — both external and internal to the company. Sometimes, sustainability is summed up as management of the "triple bottom line" — financial profitability, environmental responsibility, and social equity.

Key issues that are sometimes associated with sustainability include:

- Cleantech

- Climate change strategy

- Community and economic development

- Community capitalism

- Corporate citizenship

- Corporate governance and accountability

- Corporate social responsibility (CSR)

- Corporate–nonprofit partnerships

- Design for Environment (DfE)

- Eco-efficiency/eco-effectiveness

- Emerging markets or "Base of the Pyramid" business strategies

- Energy efficiency/strategic energy management

- Environmental footprint

- ESG (environment, social, and governance) analysis

- Fair trade

- Green building

- Green business

- Microfinance

- Natural capitalism

- Product stewardship/life-cycle analysis

Choose your definition wisely

When conducting informational interviews and applying for positions, use the company's definition of sustainability, not your own. If a company has a "corporate citizenship" program rather than a sustainability initiative, be sure the language in your cover letter reflects that. Understand what issues are — and are not — included in their definition. If you talk mostly about environmental issues, when their focus is community engagement, you may not stand out as a strong candidate.

- Social entrepreneurship

- Social enterprise

- Socially responsible investing (SRI)

- Stakeholder engagement

- Sustainable development

- Transparency

- Triple bottom line

- Workplace diversity and human rights

The ideas behind corporate sustainability have been around for some time, but the practice really began gaining ground in the 1990s. The rise of socially responsible investing and the launch in 1999 of the Dow Jones Sustainability Index raised awareness of the link between social and environmental issues and a company's financial performance. Also in 1999, the first "Beyond Grey Pinstripes" awards recognized forward-thinking business schools for incorporating social and environmental impact management topics into their curricula.

It is important to realize that sustainability is not just a strategy for risk avoidance (though it includes that). Nor is it just a public relation or marketing tactic. Sustainability can and should translate into tangible and intangible benefits for a company. Some of these benefits are summed up in Figure 1.

Companies thinking strategically about sustainability see the practice as a means to new markets, new customers, and even entirely new business models. When GE launched its "Ecomagination" campaign with a pledge to spend $1.5 billion a year on R&D for environmental technologies by 2010, CEO Jeff Immelt said he expected more than half of GE's product revenues to come from Ecomagination products by 2015. Other companies are focusing on new ways to deliver products to the world's poor — or the "Base of the Pyramid" — because they see an opportu-

Figure 1 **Opportunities for competitive advantage through sustainability**

Corporate strategy

New business models and services • Strategic competitive advantages • Organizational learning

Operations	Marketing and sales	Communi-cation	Finance and accounting	HR
• Reduced operating costs (energy, waste, raw materials) • Improved operational efficiencies • Resource productivity • Reduced liabilities	• Access to new markets, new customers • Increased sales • New product opportunities • Improved customer loyalty, brand recognition	• Improved corporate reputation • "License to operate" • Reduced political/regulatory costs	• Increased access to capital • Improved investor relations	• Employee attraction and retention • Improved productivity • Lower turnover, absenteeism, worker accidents

nity to reach entirely new (and rapidly growing) markets.

There are thousands of different ways social and environmental issues intersect with the private sector, and new sustainability applications and industries are arising every day — in big and small companies, for-profit and nonprofit organizations. As multinational corporations embrace sustainability, there are also new companies arising to provide related services and products — from those that offer sustainability consulting strategy and marketing services to those trading renewable energy credits (RECs), offering eco-friendly packaging products, or providing green retail channels. Industries like socially responsible investing, cleantech venture capital, renewable energy project development, green marketing, microfinance, social enterprise, and venture philanthropy have all been growing in recent years.

There are several excellent books on the topic of corporate sustainability and what it means both in theory and in practice for companies (a select list of the best is included in "Recommended reading" on page 141). This guide will not delve into the application of sustainable business strategies or case studies in depth. Instead, we'll focus specifically on what sustainability means for MBA career opportunities. However, in preparing for interviews, be aware that you should be well versed in sustainability theory and aware of some examples. Sustainability practitioners will expect you to be familiar with books like *Natural Capitalism*[4] and comfortable making a compelling argument for why there is a strong business case for companies to embrace sustainability.

Sustainable jobs and internship options

By now, you're wondering, "Sustainability sounds great, but are there really any *jobs* in that?" The answer is a resounding yes. In just the past five years, I have seen hundreds of sustainability-related MBA job and internship openings cross my desk. Even amid the employment challenges of the recent economic recession, hiring in certain sustainability fields like cleantech has continued to grow. Companies that see sustainability as a means to eco-efficiency and strategic competitive advantage have even more reason than ever to integrate sustainable practices.

So, what do these positions look like? Figure 2 and Figure 3 give you some ideas, ranging from renewable energy market analysts to affordable housing real estate developers. These are all actual titles held by MBA graduates in recent years. If you don't see your target companies listed here, don't worry. These lists of examples are not all-encompassing. The intention is merely to give you a better sense for the types of titles and organizations that have been hiring for sustainability-related positions.

As you can see, there are positions in nearly every industry you can imagine, with large companies, startups, nonprofits, and government. When thinking about careers, sustainability does not have to mean *corporate* sustainability. Because it is such a broad term, sustainability might include any positions that fall at the intersection of social and environmental issues and the application of business skills. For some MBAs, that means greening corporate supply chains; for others, that means using market-based solutions to deliver clean drinking water to villages in Africa.

I have no doubt that sustainability-related positions are out there for MBAs who want them. *So, here's the catch: you have to look harder for these jobs and be more creative in your networking, positioning, and negotiating to land them.* The traditional wait-

Figure 2 Example MBA internships: positions held by real MBA students

- Air Products & Chemicals, *MBA finance intern, renewable energy project*
- Asian Development Bank, *macroeconomic research and analysis intern*
- BIO Ventures for Global Health, *summer strategy analyst*
- Burt's Bees, *marketing intern*
- Calvert Social Investment Foundation, *summer intern*
- Centex Homes, *summer intern, Green Building Initiative*
- Charles Stewart Mott Foundation, *intern, Civil Society Program*
- Cherokee Investment Partners, *summer real estate associate*
- Chiquita Brands International, *corporate responsibility consultant*
- Clipper Windpower, *new project development intern*
- Coldwater Creek, Inc., *executive intern, social responsibility committee*
- Cool Earth Solar, *business development intern*
- Deloitte Touche Tohmatsu, *consultant, emerging markets*
- Discovery Communications, *strategy and development intern*
- Dow Chemical, *sustainable development consultant*
- DuPont, *strategic planning intern, renewable energy project*
- Education Pioneers, *fellow*
- Endeavor Global, *eMBA strategic consultant*
- Enterprise Social Investment Corporation, *asset management intern*
- Environmental Defense Fund, *Climate Corps MBA intern*
- Ford Motor Company, *corporate governance intern*
- GE, *Intern, Renewable Energy Leadership Program*
- Good Capital, *private equity summer associate*
- Greenfire Development, *green development intern*
- groSolar, *MBA intern*
- Innovest Strategic Value Advisors, *research analyst*

- IT Power India, *summer associate, Financial Services Group*
- KIPP, *summer fellow, marketing and development*
- Los Alamos National Laboratory, *MBA intern*
- McDonald's, *intern, supply chain/social responsibility*
- National Park Service, *business resource analyst*
- New Urban Communities, *real estate development intern*
- Population Services International (PSI), *internal consultant, Sustainable Product Department*
- Procter & Gamble, *corporate sustainable development consultant*
- Rare, *summer associate*
- Recycline Inc., *new product development intern*
- REDF, *Farber intern*
- Roche, *finance intern, Environmental Reporting Initiative*
- Seedco, *senior program associate*
- Sempra Energy, *strategic planning intern*
- ShoreBank Corporation, *summer intern*
- SJF Ventures, *venture capital fellow*
- Starbucks Coffee Co., *category management intern, US retail coffee*
- SustainAbility, *summer consulting associate*
- Sustainable Conservation, *hospitality and tourism strategy intern*
- The Conservation Fund, *real estate associate*
- The Cook Center for Sustainable Agriculture in the American West, *consultant, business development*
- The Hitachi Foundation, *Yoshiyama Business in Society fellow*
- The Timberland Company, *marketing intern*
- The Walt Disney Company, *graduate associate, International Labor Standards Group*
- TransFair USA, *category management MBA fellow*
- USAID, *public–private alliance builder*
- Wal-Mart, *Sustainability Energy Group intern*
- Wells Fargo, *intern, community development*
- World Business Council for Sustainable Development, *summer intern*

Figure 3 Example full-time positions: titles held by real MBA graduates in recent years

- ABN AMRO, *Socially Responsible Investing Analyst*
- B Lab, *Standards & Capital Markets Associate*
- Bank of America, *Senior Vice President, Corporate Workplace, Environmental Risk and Sustainability Group*
- Bioenergy Development Fund, *Associate*
- Bill and Melinda Gates Foundation, *Senior Financial Analyst*
- Blu Skye Sustainability Consulting, *Senior Consultant*
- Brazilian Council for Sustainable Development, *Advisor to the Executive President*
- Burt's Bees, *Brand Manager, U.S. Marketing*
- Business for Social Responsibility, *Director, Advisory Services*
- Calvert Group, *Senior Social Research Analyst*
- Chicago Climate Exchange, *Economist*
- Chevron, *Senior Biofuels Analyst*
- Citigroup, *Manager of Environmental Affairs*
- City Year, *Senior Corporate Partnerships Manager*
- College Summit, *Director, National Partnerships & Investments*
- Community Energy, *Marketing Director*
- Corporate Executive Board, *Strategic Research Consultant*
- DOMANI LLC, *Sustainability Consultant*
- eBay, Inc., *Manager, Global Citizenship*
- EcoAmerica, *Vice President, Development*
- Eco-Libris, *Co-Founder*
- Education Pioneers, *Managing Director*
- EnerNOC, *Corporate Development Analyst*
- Enterprise Social Investment Corporation, *Development Officer*
- Environmental Defense Fund, *Marketing & Communications Manager*
- Ethical Marketplace, *Host and Writer*
- GE, *Renewable Energy Leadership Program*
- Generation Investment Management, *Associate*
- GlobalGiving, *Business Development Manager*
- Green Village, *Vice President*
- Hewlett-Packard, *Business Development — Emerging Markets*
- ICF Consulting, *Senior Associate*
- Ideal Bite, *Founder*
- Interface FLOR, *Manager of Sustainable Strategy*
- Investors' Circle, *Director, Business Development*
- John Deere, *Market Information Manager, Wind Energy*
- Johnson & Johnson, *Associate, Procurement Leadership Development Program*
- Kinetix, LLC, *Strategist, Sustainability Consulting*
- KLD Research & Analytics, *Investment Analyst*
- KPMG International, *Director, Global Green*
- McKesson Corporation, *Director, Corporate Citizenship*
- Mercy Housing, *Affordable Housing Real Estate Developer*
- Microsoft Corporation, *Product Manager, Emerging Markets*
- Natural Resources Defense Council, *Associate, Center for Market Transformation*
- NextEra Energy Resources, *Renewable Energy Brand Manager*
- Novozymes North America, *Biofuels Specialist*
- Population Services International, *International Fellow*
- Reebok, *Human Rights Assistant Manager*
- Schaefer & Associates, *Socially Responsible Financial Advisor*
- Shell Wind Energy, *Business Development Manager*
- SolarDock, *Vice President, Marketing & Administration*
- Sun Microsystems, *Director, Corporate Sustainability and Responsibility*
- SunEdison, LLC, *Marketing Services Manager*
- Sustainable Value Partners, *Consultant*
- Target Corporation, *Senior Business Analyst, Global Compliance*
- The Conservation Fund, *Corporate Development Associate*
- The Rockefeller Foundation, *Program Coordinator*
- The Timberland Company, *Social Enterprise Manager*
- Trillium Asset Management Corporation, *Assistant Portfolio Manager*
- Unilever, *Associate Brand Manager*
- U.S. Green Building Council, *Manager, Commercial Real Estate*
- Vantage Point Venture Partners, *Vice President, Cleantech*
- Vivavi, *Founder and CEO*
- Wal-Mart, *Senior Manager of Energy Services*
- Whole Foods, *Distribution System Team Leader*
- World Resources Institute, *Senior Manager, Markets & Sustainable Enterprise*
- WWF, *Senior Program Officer, Business & Industry*
- Yahoo! For Good, *Senior Manager*

and-the-job-will-come-to-me model of on-campus MBA recruiting rarely works for these types of positions. For those who are willing to put in the effort, though, the payoff of working in your dream job is worth it.

MBA careers in sustainability: a framework

You are probably beginning to understand just how diverse the potential applications of sustainability are. In fact, the challenge with sustainability careers is typically not one of finding options, but rather of focusing your job search. With so many different industries and organizations working on so many different environmental and social issues, narrowing down job search targets can be thoroughly overwhelming. What's more, most sustainability-related openings are not going to come to you through on-campus recruiting, so you are going to have to know what you want to do and go after it yourself. Where to begin?

As with any career search, it is critically important to have a clear focus in your sustainability job search. You need to know, and be able to articulate, what kind of position you're looking for, where you want to work, and why. In the following pages, I'll give you two ways to think about focusing your sustainable career search. The first helps you think about your career function, and the second helps you think about what type of organization and role you're interested in.

Career function

The first step in thinking about your career options is to identify which functional discipline most interests you, and then determine how sustainability might apply. MBA jobs related to sustainability cross all industries, job functions, and organizational types. While some companies do have corporate sustainability or CSR departments, more often sustainability is not a separate job functional area — like finance, marketing, or operations management — but rather a "lens" through which you can look at a company and your role within it.

For example, an MBA student looking at finance career functions through the lens of sustainability might pursue careers in socially responsible investing (SRI) or environmental, social, and governance (ESG) investment analysis. A student interested in marketing, on the other hand, might look at careers related to green marketing, social marketing, or cause marketing.

What functional discipline interests you most, and how might sustainability be applied? Figure 4 summarizes some of the sustainability applications/skills associated with different MBA functional disciplines.

You might start by thinking about which of your core MBA classes you have enjoyed most. Are you excited about the work you've done in your core strategy classes? Are you planning to concentrate in a particular area like marketing or supply chain? Which clubs have you been most active in? Do you gravitate towards a particular discipline?

No matter what the job, your employer will expect you to have strong MBA fundamentals and depth in one or more specific functional areas. Sustainability is not a separate discipline, but rather a way of bringing MBA tools and analysis to bear on complex social and environmental challenges, so a rigorous background in your MBA disciplines is fundamental.

Lastly, note that Figure 4 helps you think about skill sets, but it does not necessarily specify your role or job title within an organization. For instance, CSR/sustainability strategy as a skill might be applied either as a member of a corporate sustainability department internal to a company, or as an external consul-

Tip for career changers

Many MBA students are career changers, so it is not necessarily expected that your pre-MBA work experience will match your post-MBA aspirations. However, if changing careers, it is important that you fill any functional gaps on your resume while in school. So, for instance, if you intend to move into marketing, but don't have any pre-MBA work experience in marketing, be sure to build a compelling story by not only taking marketing classes, but also tackling projects, internships, or volunteer opportunities related to marketing.

Figure 4 **Sustainability-related applications by MBA discipline**

MBA discipline	Sustainable applications/skills
Corporate strategy	• Corporate social responsibility (CSR)/sustainability strategy • Competitive advantage through sustainability • Strategic positioning • Sustainable R&D investment strategy • Business planning for sustainable ventures or social enterprises • Emerging market and "Base of the Pyramid" business strategies
Finance and accounting	• Sustainability/CSR metrics and reporting • Socially responsible investing (SRI) • ESG investment analysis • Community/economic development finance • Risk management • Full-cost accounting/environmental accounting • Corporate governance & reporting • Social return on investment (SROI) analysis
Marketing	• Brand management for socially and environmentally responsible brands • New market development and new product development for sustainable technologies, products, services • Design for Environment (DfE) • Market entry in emerging markets/"Base of the Pyramid" marketing • Social marketing • Cause marketing
Operations/ supply chain	• Responsible supply chain, vendor codes of conduct, and management systems • Managing for environmental efficiency and pollution prevention • Product stewardship/life-cycle management/ product takeback • Social impact management • Innovative distribution strategies • Sustainable business practice integration • Supply chain optimization
Leading and managing	• Responsible corporate governance • Sustainability visioning and organizational change • Strategic and ethical human resources practices • Stakeholder engagement, community relations, corporate stewardship • Social venture management

tant with a sustainability consulting firm. Business planning for sustainable or social ventures might be done as an entrepreneur yourself, working for a startup company, or working on new initiatives within a larger company. So, your next step will be to think more about organization and role.

Organization and role

Once you identify what functional discipline interests you most, and how sustainability might be overlaid with that discipline, there are still many different ways you could be employed. That leads us to the second way of narrowing your focus — organization and role. You need to examine whether it is most important to you to work for a "sustainable" organization, or to have a sustainability-related job function, or both.

Consider the options presented in Figure 5.

Along the **horizontal axis**, the designation "Traditional" organization represents the kind of firms that have historically conducted on-campus recruiting for MBA graduates — for instance, large multinational corporations, investment banks, management consulting firms, etc. In the second column, a "Sustainability-oriented" organization represents an organization that has an environmental or social focus as central to its core mission, product, or service. These might include, for example, an organic/natural product company, renewable energy company, sustainability consulting firm, social enterprise, or nonprofit organization. Sometimes these types of organizations are termed "mission-driven" organizations or "values-based" companies. In general, they tend to be smaller and more entrepreneurial than the firms in the Traditional category, and may not have a history of recruiting MBAs through on-campus recruiting channels — in fact, may not have a history of hiring MBAs at all.

The **vertical axis** differentiates between the types of roles you might hold within the firm. Are you seeking a "Traditional" MBA

Figure 5 **Sustainable MBA careers matrix**

Company/organization

	Traditional	**Sustainability-oriented**
Traditional	**Examples** • Financial Analyst, **Intel** • Consultant, **McKinsey** • Senior Brand Manager, **Coca-Cola**	**Examples** • Marketing Manager, **Burt's Bees** • Operations Officer, **Good Capital** • Real Estate Developer, **Mercy Housing**
Sustainability-oriented	**Examples** • Environmental Manager, **Citigroup** • CSR Associate, **Nike** • Sustainable Product Manager, **Johnson & Johnson**	**Examples** • Trailblazer, **Knowledge is Power Program (KIPP)** • Sustainable Enterprise Program Manager, **World Resources Institute** • Sustainability Analyst, **Blu Skye**

Job/role

job title — for instance, chief financial officer (CFO), brand manager, or supply chain analyst? Or are you seeking a "Sustainability-oriented" job that involves managing social/environmental issues as a primary part of your daily function — for instance, as a socially responsible investing analyst, environmental manager, or CSR manager?

Figure 5 also gives some concrete examples for each type of organization and role. These examples are all actual titles held by recent MBA grads who are pursuing sustainability-related careers.

Which quadrant of this matrix interests you most? Do you want to spend the majority of your day working on sustainability or CSR issues? Or, is it more important to you to be working at a values-driven organization, regardless of your role there? Do you see yourself working at a multinational company, helping to change the organization from within? Or, do you prefer a more entrepreneurial environment?

This is a useful way to begin to focus your job search. It will also help you map your strategy, since your job search strategy will vary greatly depending on which of these quadrants you focus on. If you are interested primarily in sustainability-oriented organizations, for instance, you will likely need to focus more efforts on an independent (or "off-campus") search than on-campus recruiting.

For each of the quadrants of this matrix, the types of positions you will pursue will vary, so let's discuss them one by one.

Traditional role in a traditional company

"Traditional role in a traditional company" is one career option that many sustainability-oriented MBAs want to skip over. However, it's worth some serious consideration, because for many MBAs, the best path to a meaningful sustainability job is through a traditional MBA role. There are many powerful ways to effect change and integrate sustainability from within a traditional MBA role. Sometimes the *most* effective way to implement sustainability practices is in a front-line role such as product manager or procurement manager where you are in a position to integrate sustainability considerations into daily operational decisions directly.

Traditional MBA roles also afford you a chance to learn the company's core business and then integrate sustainability into the business in a new way. Some MBAs have taken this approach and ultimately created a new niche for themselves from inside the company — for instance, as a sustainable marketing expert or green procurement specialist. Others have spent some time in a traditional role, building their skill set and learning best industry practices, and then moved to a sustainability organization later in their career. Even mission-driven companies, for instance, recognize the value of a traditional consumer-packaged goods (CPG) marketing background, and seek out professionals with that kind of training.

Lastly, your sustainability skills and interests can be an important differentiator for you in an interview for traditional positions. Many recruiters recognize that sustainably-minded MBAs are thinking strategically and creatively about the real global issues facing companies. An understanding of the complex environmental and social management challenges facing companies, combined with MBA business fundamentals, can only help your candidacy.

Traditional positions are, of course, the ones that employers typically hire MBAs for through on-campus recruiting, so this resource guide will not delve much into specific job search strategies in this category. For positions in this category, use all the on-campus resources at your disposal. In interviews, some recruiters will be familiar with sustainability, but others will not, so avoid buzzwords and be prepared to explain your interest in the topic in very bottom-line-focused terminology. You want to demonstrate that your understanding of sustainability makes you a savvy, informed, and well-rounded candidate, but not an activist or critic.

Sustainability-oriented role in a traditional company

Jobs in the category of "sustainability-oriented role in a traditional company" are, for many MBAs, some of the most desirable sustainability roles. These are positions in corporate sustainability or CSR departments at major multinational companies, financial institutions, or management consulting firms. A title like Sustainability Director or CSR Manager of a major multinational company is alluring, because it implies a great detail of opportunity to lead change on sustainability issues in the private sector. It's easy to see why MBA students gravitate towards these roles.

Of course, these are also some of the hardest positions to identify and obtain. Corporate sustainability and CSR departments are small, and competition for these positions is fierce. And, these positions aren't for everyone. They sometimes require a great deal of "swimming upstream" in trying to change a company.

These positions are not impossible to come by, but they do require a very persistent and focused job search. Much of this guide is devoted to these types of roles. Part II includes sections on CSR and corporate sustainability jobs in greater detail, along with example job titles, employers, career search tips, and profiles of MBA graduates who are working in these roles. The resources in Part III will also be helpful in your job search for a sustainability position in a traditional company.

Traditional role in a sustainability-oriented organization

The category of "Traditional role in a sustainability-oriented organization" represents a large set of job opportunities in roles such as marketing manager, financial officer, and operations director for sustainability-focused companies and nonprofit organizations. You will, of course, have to further define what type of organization or industry you want to focus on, but the important distinction to make first is: do I want to be helping a big company become more sustainable, or do I want to be helping advance an organization whose entire focus is sustainability?

Organizations in this category cross many industries — sustainability consulting, organic or natural consumer products, renewable/alternative energy, socially responsible investing, green building, environmental conservation, or microfinance — to name a few. These might be nonprofit organizations, for-profit ventures, or hybrids of both (for example, social enterprises or B corporations).

If you choose to work in a sustainability-oriented organization, you will probably be surrounded by like-minded individuals who all share a fundamental knowledge of, and support for, the social or environmental objective at hand. On the other hand, you may not have the same kinds of resources as at a large corporation.

The job search resources in this category depend on how you further refine your industry focus. Parts II and III of this guide will give you a wide range of ideas and career search specifics for jobs in this category.

Sustainability-oriented role in a sustainability-oriented organization

The most difficult-to-categorize jobs are in the category of "Sustainability-oriented role in a sustainability-oriented organization." These positions vary greatly by organization and industry, and might range from a position pricing environmental risk for a sustainable investment firm, to a role managing a social marketing campaign for an international development organization.

The options here often depend on the particular needs of a specialized industry or niche market. For instance, organizations devoted to organic agriculture, green product retailing, or micro-lending would all have very particular, and very different, types of roles for MBAs. Students interested in this category usually have a particular industry that they are targeting, and a corresponding skill set to offer. If you know which industry you are interested in, you can research the industry and talk to professionals to get a better sense for organizational structures and career paths.

Part II of this guide covers career paths in socially responsible investing, green marketing, sustainability consulting, and other fields that could fall in this category. Part III gives you further sustainability career research tools, reading lists, and websites that can help your job search in this category.

Next steps

Using this matrix to refine your personal job search focus is a great first step because it directly informs your job search strategy. If your focus is on traditional companies, the types of research you'll do and individuals you'll network with will be different from that of a search focused on sustainability-oriented organizations. No matter which quadrant suits you best, though, there are opportunities to advance the practice of sustainability and make sustainability the focus of a rewarding career for you.

A note about salaries

I am often asked, understandably, whether taking a sustainability-related position means taking a pay cut. Most full-time MBAs are graduating with a mountain of debt — not to mention lost salary from their time in the program — and are counting on a big salary bump in their post-MBA careers. I have found that many MBAs working in sustainability careers *do* make less than their peers, but not necessarily for the reasons you'd expect. Salary has more to do with the *organization* than the job function.

As a general rule, big companies hire more MBAs and pay more in starting salaries than small companies, startup ventures, and nonprofit organizations. This applies to sustainability professionals and other executives alike. In a 2006 salary survey of corporate citizenship professionals, the median salary range was $90,000–99,999. Forty-four per cent of the respondents said their salary was the same or higher than that of other employees at a similar level in other departments in their company (33% said they didn't know, and only 22% said their salary was lower).[5]

If you pursue a sustainability or CSR position at a big company like Bayer or GE, you should expect a salary in line with other MBA positions at that company. On the other hand, students who choose to work at a smaller firm, entrepreneurial venture, or nonprofit organization should expect lower salaries — regardless of whether it's a sustainability-related job or not. So, when

> ## Balancing starting salary with long-term goals
>
> "If you're targeting a small company, you may need to take a lower position and pay than you would take elsewhere, but if you're patient and you position yourself correctly, you may end up with a much more interesting and much more fulfilling career. This is hard to accept when you're surrounded by classmates who are getting big signing bonuses and huge salaries, but it's much better in the long run."
>
> *Natacha Kiler (MBA 2007), Marketing Services Manager, SunEdison*

benchmarking your job offer against your peers' offers, be sure to compare apples to apples. You shouldn't expect less for a sustainability position per se, but you should expect a job in a nonprofit organization or startup company to pay less than one with a major corporation.

Finally, it's worth reiterating that salary is only one factor among many in your career decision. There are many great reasons for choosing to work at a nonprofit, startup, or smaller values-driven company. Besides job satisfaction, there are other tangible and intangible benefits these organizations might offer you — from better work–life balance to paid community service days, extra vacation, or even company equity.

As many MBA alumni will attest, the reward of doing a job you love at an organization you are completely committed to is worth more than money. Some individuals thrive in entrepreneurial environments, others need the structure of a big company or the mission-oriented nature of a nonprofit. Spend your time finding the right role for you at the right organization for you.

More on salaries

- "Profile of the Profession 2006: Salary Information," Boston College Center for Corporate Citizenship, 2006 (results from a survey of 748 professionals working in corporate citizenship and community involvement; www.bcccc.net, under "Career Center")

- "CSR Jobs Report 2008," study of 1,255 CSR job postings by Ellen Weinreb and Net Impact; www.ellenweinreb.com/Guidance.html

- "The CSR Salary Survey, 2008/2009," UK-based salary survey sponsored by Acre Resources Ltd, Acona CMG, and Ethical Performance; www.csrsalarysurvey.com

Tips for an off-campus job search

Because of the nature of sustainability positions, you may find that you need to conduct an "off-campus" or "independent" job search, rather than relying exclusively on on-campus recruiting activities. Many MBA students find the prospect of off-campus job searches to be daunting, but these searches are incredibly valuable in many ways — often even more valuable than on-campus recruiting activities. Think about it this way: when you're conducting an off-campus job search, you are not just meeting recruiting prospects for your next job; you are *building your personal network for life.*

The contacts that you make in an off-campus search have the potential to be your future mentors, business partners, suppliers, or collaborators in your post-MBA career. Even when they do not yield an immediate job lead, the contacts that you make in an off-campus search often have jobs to offer you further down the road. Keep in mind that the field of sustainability is still small compared to, say, investment banking or consumer marketing. You'll find that, if you make a good impression with influential people in your chosen field, it will open many doors among the industry. You may not know how or when the relationships will pay off, but if you build a strong network during your off-campus search, it is likely to pay dividends in your long-term career.

Also, contrary to popular opinion, off-campus searching does not necessarily demand any more energy or time than preparing well for on-campus recruiting activities. While your MBA classmates might spend hours attending

> **Building your network**
>
> "Don't be shy about informational interviewing — it is so common in the field. You will often find that you end up working with a lot of the people you talk to in those interviews. Also, don't underestimate the power of your network in helping you to get a job, and in helping you as a resource once you have a job."
>
> *Val Smith (MBA 2002), Vice President, Corporate Sustainability, Citigroup*

investment banking networking events or practicing consulting case interviews, you should devote the same level of effort and attention to conducting informational interviews, attending industry events, and building an off-campus network.

Some tips for conducting an off-campus search focused on sustainability careers:

- **Read extensively about the latest industry news and sustainability issues in your chosen field.** Use this research to develop a list of target companies, relevant contacts at those companies, and informed questions for informational interviews. The field of sustainability is evolving every day, so it's essential that you are up to speed on the latest news and trends (recommended reading lists and website resources are included throughout Parts II and III of this guide)

- **Join Net Impact.** Net Impact (www.netimpact.org) is a global organization devoted specifically to business students and professionals interested in sustainability. Their job board, career resources, and networking opportunities are well worth the annual membership fee. Search the global member database to reach out to professionals working in fields you're interested in

- **Join industry-specific groups and listservs.** If you have a particular industry focus, join industry trade associations — for instance, the US Green Building Council or American Wind Energy Association. Many trade associations have position papers and research resources available to members; some even have member-specific career resources or job boards. Review the member directory and note who is speaking at association events to build a list of contacts

- **Attend important industry conferences to network**, even if it means traveling to do so. For example, attend the Business for Social Responsibility (BSR) Annual Conference, the Sustainable Brands conference, or Co-op America's Green Business Conference. (See "Relevant events" on page 136 for more ideas.) If you ask far enough in advance, you might be able to secure a place as a conference volunteer in lieu of paying registration fees

- **Develop local networks.** If you have a specific geographic focus, look for local sustainability-related groups in that area. These might be professional groups like the Sustainable Practice Network in New York, social networking groups like the North Carolina Sustainability Network on LinkedIn, or nonprofit organizations like Sustainable Seattle. Subscribe to the newsletters for groups in your target area and attend events when possible. Pay attention to which companies and individuals are participating in events or receiving recognition, and seek out meetings with them. Many cities or regions have sustainable business awards and/or green business certification programs; look at the list of companies that have been recognized in years past for additional targets

- **Leverage social networking sites.** Seek out online social networking groups like the "CSR Jobs" group on Yahoo!, the "Green Jobs & Career Network" group on LinkedIn, or the "Sustainable MBA" group on Facebook.com

- **Visit sustainable job posting sites.** Read past job postings to identify which types of job titles you are interested in and well suited for, what skills are required, and which companies have been hiring for these types of positions. (See the list of job posting websites on page 143 for some ideas.) Consider how you can fill any gaps on your resume and position yourself for these types of openings in the future

> **Set up search agents.** Create search agents using keywords (for instance, "MBA and sustainability") on meta-search websites like SimplyHired.com and JustMeans.com. These sites will then automatically email any new openings to you that meet your criteria. Similarly, you can often create online "job alerts" on the websites of any companies or organizations you're interested in

- **Use all of your personal networks.** It should go without saying that the best contacts to start with for an off-campus search (sustainability or otherwise) are those in your established network. Start with the alumni of both your MBA program and your undergraduate institution. Talk to professors, MBA classmates, friends, family, and other colleagues for ideas

- **Request informational interviews with contacts at companies of interest.** Informational interviews can be a great way not only to learn but also to network. See "Making the Most of Informational Interviews" next, for more on the topic

In talking with MBA alumni who have successfully found sustainability positions, a few themes emerge again and again — be **entrepreneurial** in your search, be **flexible**, and be **persistent**. Your job search will be different from that of your MBA classmates pursuing traditional positions. It may require more patience, more resourcefulness, and more follow-up. Job offers will probably come later in the year and may take some creative design on your part.

But the reward — working in a career that you are truly passionate about — is worth it, and the network that you build during your job search will be an important asset as your career progresses.

Making the most of informational interviews

When asked how to network in this field, informational interviews are by far the most-cited answer among alumni interviewed for this guide. Nearly every MBA graduate interviewed had a story to tell about a sustainability internship or job offer that came as a direct or indirect result of an informational interview. Because the sustainability circles are so small, conducting a professional and meaningful informational interview with a contact can make a huge difference in opening doors for you throughout the field.

Most sustainability practitioners, though busy, are happy to make time for informational interviews with MBA students when they can. Once you have their ear, though, there are a few ways to stand out and leave a memorable impression with contacts. "Be prepared," says Rebecca Swartz (MBA 2005), a CSR Compliance Specialist at a major retailer who honed her skills conducting more than 20 informational interviews as a student. "Conduct the interview at a high level with good-quality questions that show that you already know something about the field but are also willing to learn."

"A lot of the informational interviews I do are kind of flat, very generic," says Lindsay James (MBA 2003), Director of Strategic Sustainability with the sustainable carpet manufacturer Interface. "The ones I love are more meaningful discussions. For instance, if a student says, 'I was working on a project at my company and thought about applying sustainability in this new way. What do you think? Have you tried something like that?' It really becomes a good thought exercise."

Other discussion-provoking questions you might ask include:

- Where do you see the field going in the next 2–5 years?

- What skills do you think are most important for individuals working in this space?

- What's your advice for someone getting started in this field?

If there are new developments happening in the industry — for instance, a pending climate legislation bill or a new fair trade certification standard — ask about how this might affect the company or the industry as a whole. And always close the conversation with, "What other companies or individuals do you think I should be talking to?" Ideally, you'll end every informational interview with two or three new contacts.

Another important tip in conducting informational interviews is to clearly define your sustainability focus. Have your interests narrowed down to one or two specific paths that you can articulate. This will help the person understand how she can help you. When you say, "I'm willing to do anything; I just know I want to work in sustainability," you may think you are being flexible, but you may actually be making it harder to help. "I don't know where to go with 'anything,' " says Katherine Neebe (MBA 2004), a Senior Program Officer with WWF. When a student can define his functional interests, industry, or geographical focus, it is easier to direct him to specific resources and contacts.

It is also possible (though less common) to define your interests too narrowly. Often, this has to do with geographic preference. If a student says, for instance, that her goal is to work in green marketing for a major consumer packaged goods company in Portland, Oregon, then her options are going to be drastically limited. If you have a specific geographic focus, be prepared to be flexible in considering jobs in the context of the industries and companies prevalent in that market.

While you've undoubtedly heard these all before, some other tips for informational interviews bear repeating:

- **Know what kind of help you are looking for from each contact.** Are you asking them for introductions to other contacts? Industry-specific information? General background information? You never want to ask for a job outright in an informational interview — keep the conversation focused on advice and other resources

- **Show that you've done your homework.** While your contact won't expect you to be an expert on their business, they will expect you to have done at least some basic research on the company or industry. Avoid, for instance, asking fundamental questions about a company's sustainability initiatives when its sustainability report is posted on its website

- **Be sincere.** Ask questions that will be truly helpful to you in your career search. The professionals you're talking with can tell the difference between someone who is just going through the motions or asking textbook or "coached" questions for the sake of a contact and someone who is genuinely interested in the answers

- **Be conscientious of your contact's time.** Rebecca Swartz advises, "If you tell someone at the outset that the call will take 20 minutes of his time, then when you get to the 20-minute mark, say, 'I still have a few questions, but I want to be aware of your time. We are at the 20-minute point now.' If he wants to give you more time, he has the opportunity, but you shouldn't assume that"

- **Send timely and thoughtful thank-you notes.** This seems like such a small thing, and is easy to overlook, but rest assured that recruiters and executives *do* pay attention to thank you notes

- **Follow up in a few weeks.** If you request informational interviews and your contacts don't respond immediately, remember that they might just be busy, not unwilling. Don't assume the answer is "no," when they may just be behind on email. If you send an email, wait two weeks and then try calling or emailing to follow up

Finally, the best thing you can do to stand out in an informational interview is to bring some insights or connections of value to the relationship. For instance, if you spoke with a contact in the fall and want to follow up a few months later, you might email with, "I saw this interesting new McKinsey study on the costs and benefits of climate change mitigation measures, and it reminded me of our conversation. I thought I'd share it with you in case you haven't seen it yet." Or, "When we spoke, I told you about a white paper I was working on about social return on investment. I thought you might like to see the final product. Please feel free to share it with anyone else in your company who might find it interesting. I'd also be happy to answer questions or share details of the project."

> ### Taking a risk
>
> "I was always one who would put myself out there. My mindset was, if you don't ask, you're never going to get. That helped me in a lot of situations."
>
> *Jay Carlis (MBA 2007), Marketing Director, Community Energy*

One of the advantages of being a student is that you are on top of the very latest methodologies, case studies, and research on sustainability topics. Don't underestimate the value of this. Busy executives might read the *Wall Street Journal* and Greenbiz.com, but often don't have enough time, or access, to read academic publications or research studies. Your insight in sending them a new and relevant article or report can be a real differentiator.

Gaining experience

Another theme that emerges in talking with MBA alumni who are working in sustainability careers is the importance of relevant real-world experience. At first blush, this can sound discouraging to students who are career changers trying to break into a new industry or discipline. But real-world experience does not necessarily have to mean pre-MBA work experience. You can leverage your time as a student to gain that experience — whether through an internship, class project, or extracurricular activity.

Standing out from the crowd

"The biggest disadvantage everyone has today in sustainability is that everyone is interested in it, but very few people actually have experience in it."

Michelle Chislett (MBA 2006), Vice President, Solar Project Development Group, SkyPower

Think creatively about how you can maximize your time as a student. The goal is to have a compelling story to tell in an interview about why you are interested in a particular career path and industry, and evidence to back it up. Below are a few ideas.

Internships

As you undoubtedly know, the most direct way to build your experience in a particular field is through an internship. Besides summer internships, some students also accept part-time internships during the academic year or over winter break. Even short-term or unpaid internships are a great way to add another industry or organization name to your resume, and open networking doors for you. Internships are also a way to demonstrate your value to a company; once you've worked for an organization, they are more likely to be motivated to keep you on or help you in your job search.

Research projects

More than half of the MBA alumni profiled in this guide tell a career story that started with a research project they worked on as a student. "The best thing that I saw students do in school was use class projects to pursue a research question or project that interested them, but that they could easily share with and create value for companies," says Libby Reder (MBA 2006), Head of Environmental Initiatives at eBay.

Research projects might be in-depth independent study projects, practicum or consulting projects, masters' theses, white papers, or end-of-term deliverables for a class. Projects are incredibly powerful opportunities in terms of both opening doors with contacts and producing expertise of value to potential employers. If there is a company that you are really compelled to work for, consider calling them and pitching a project idea.

You can also use benchmarking studies or industry analysis projects as a reason to call a broad spectrum of practitioners and interview them for the study. For example, "Hello. I'm an MBA student working on a study of sustainability practices in the healthcare industry. If you have 15 minutes of time, I'd like to interview you for the project. In return, I will share the final study with you."

Extracurricular activities

Extracurricular activities will probably not gain you as much credit in the experience category as research projects or internships, but can still go a long way towards building your credibility and your story with prospective employers. Consider participating in a Board Fellows program, if your school has one, or take a leadership role with your Net Impact chapter. Organizing a conference or panel discussion on a sustainability-related topic for a business school club is another great door-opener with contacts. If you intend to pursue a career in social entrepreneurship or environmental conservation, volunteering with a local non-profit organization will help demonstrate your commitment to the cause.

Authoring an article or a blog can be another great way to gain knowledge and contacts in the field while also creating something of value to share with companies. "There was one jobseeker who came to see me who had a blog about CSR. She used the blog as a way to gain access to professionals in the field, whom she interviewed," says Reder. "And then, of course, she could also use the blog as a demonstration of her work. It was really smart."

Katherine Neebe (MBA 2004), Senior Program Officer at WWF, suggests:

> Many schools are also beginning to develop sustainability plans at the business school and/or on the larger campus. It may be that there are opportunities to consult on these projects and lead individual initiatives. Furthermore, this latter work may allow a student to gain considerable insight into the reality of implementing sustainability and its associated challenges — a skill set that is likely to translate to the private sector or sustainability consulting companies.

Finally, be selective. You don't have to do it *all*. Choose projects and experiences that are focused and aligned with your career objectives. Projects should be ones you can turn into a compelling story in an interview. Before signing up for a club or a practicum project, think about how you will talk about that decision to prospective employers, and how it will help position you for the job you want after graduation.

Plan B?

You really want a sustainability-related career, but you wonder if you should pursue a "traditional" MBA recruiting path as a backup plan. Is this the right strategy? Do you have time for parallel job searches? Will your heart be in it?

Most career services offices will tell you to pursue simultaneous job searches, interviewing for traditional MBA jobs on campus while also applying for sustainability roles. They argue that there are not enough sustainability-focused jobs and you may be disappointed with the salaries or won't find a sustainability position at all.

This might be the right approach for some individuals, particularly if you have a nonprofit or government background and want to build some strong business fundamentals in the private sector. If you think you would be excited to work in a traditional MBA role and bring your sustainability skills to bear there, even better.

On the other hand, if you are really committed to working in a sustainability-focused job, this might not be the right approach. Some MBA graduates working in sustainability careers will tell you they never could have done it if they had a Plan B. "Having a 'backup strategy' by interviewing for traditional positions can backfire on you," says Rebecca Swartz. "What happens is, you get an offer in the fall and then you have to decide whether or not to take it. If you take it, chances are you'll end up unhappy, because it's not what you really want to do. Then you've just taken the offer away from one of your classmates, and given yourself a hard decision to make."

Many MBAs who are successful at landing the CSR or sustainability position of their dreams commit 100% to the sustainability job search. They know what they want to do, and spend all their time and energy going after it. That does not mean blind optimism. These MBAs do their research and pay their dues. Instead of attending company presentations on campus, they spend their time conducting informational interviews and networking at external events. They develop a realistic understanding of what kinds of roles exist, and how they can add value to the organization and the field of sustainability. And, they are aware that their career path may mean a lower starting salary than that of their colleagues, and that the offers will come later in the year.

So, spend some time soul-searching and decide what you really want from your job search. Whichever route you take — traditional or sustainability — pursue it with focus, intent, and dedication. "Pursue something you love, pursue something you're good at, and weave sustainability in," says Marc Major (MBA 2004), Co-Founder and Principal, Cleargreen Advisors. "Think big. Think beyond yourself."

Part II

Navigating specific career paths

Because MBA career paths related to sustainability cover such a broad range of functions and industries, it is impossible to offer a set of career resources without further narrowing the discipline into fields of interest. The following pages offer industry- and role-specific resources for some of these fields. This is by no means an exhaustive list of career possibilities, but is intended to address the sectors of highest interest among MBA students.

The next sections include:

- Corporate social responsibility (CSR)
- Corporate environmental management/corporate sustainability
- Sustainability consulting
- Green building/sustainable real estate development
- Renewable energy industry jobs
- Socially responsible investing (SRI)
- Environmental conservation/nonprofits
- Social entrepreneurship
- Green marketing
- Additional career paths

Each of these sections walks through some of the key industry issues and trends, along with specific career search notes and tips compiled from interviews with professionals in these roles. To give you a sense for some of the career path options, I've included lists of example employers and example job titles from recently advertised openings. These sections also spotlight some of the best informational resources for careers in the field and share a real-world story of an MBA graduate working in a related role.

The goal is to paint a picture not only of what the jobs look like, but also give you practical advice on how to search for opportunities and stand out as a candidate.

Corporate social responsibility (CSR)

Keywords

Corporate responsibility, corporate social responsibility (CSR), corporate citizenship, community engagement, stakeholder management

Example employers

Nike, Starbucks, Gap, Adidas, Walt Disney, Wal-Mart, Chiquita, Pfizer, Mattel, Bureau Veritas, Fair Labor Association, Cameron-Cole, TransFair, International Labour Office (ILO); CSR auditing/compliance consulting firms, *Fortune* 500 companies

Areas of focus

CSR strategy, management, and reporting; Labor standards monitoring and compliance; Public relations/community relations; Corporate philanthropy; Community service program management; Corporate philanthropy; Stakeholder engagement

Skills needed

Change management; Organizational behavior; Communications; Strategy; Project management; Leading, motivating, and training personnel

Key resources

- Boston College Center for Corporate Citizenship, www.bcccc.net (see Career Center)
- Business for Social Responsibility (BSR), www.bsr.org (see especially Research Reports and CSR Jobs pages)
- CSRwire, www.csrwire.com
- Ellen Weinreb, www.ellenweinreb.com
- Ethical Corporation, www.ethicalcorp.com
- Net Impact, www.netimpact.org

Main issues

There are several definitions of corporate social responsibility or CSR but, in general, the term refers to a company's responsibility to manage its impacts on society at large. One concise definition is:

> Corporate social responsibility is the notion that corporations have an obligation to constituent groups in society other than stockholders and beyond that prescribed by law or union contract.[6]

The specific issues may vary depending on which organization is doing the defining, but CSR often refers to the management of many or all of the following:

- Corporate citizenship initiatives

- Corporate giving/philanthropy

- Labor standards and human rights in the supply chain

- Corporate governance and ethics

- Community engagement

- Stakeholder engagement (i.e., interaction with a broad range of customers, suppliers, community groups, and others affected by the business)

- Product responsibility (supply chain/production)

Depending on the company, CSR may or may not include environmental responsibility. When it does, the term is sometimes used interchangeably with "sustainability" or "triple bottom line" business. CSR may also be used interchangeably with the term "corporate responsibility," or just plain "social responsibility."

CSR has gained attention — particularly among large companies — in the last decade. Global corporations especially are increasingly receiving pressure from customers, non-governmental organizations (NGOs), and other constituents to be more transparent about and, accountable for, their social and environmental impacts. More and more corporations are creating CSR departments, producing annual CSR or corporate citizenship reports, and participating in voluntary CSR organizations and initiatives.

According to a 2006 McKinsey survey of executives on business and society, 84% of global business executives believe that the role of the corporation is to "generate high returns to investors but *balance with contributions to the broader public good.*"[7] A 2008 KPMG survey revealed that nearly 80% of the largest 250 companies in the world now issue corporate responsibility reports — up from 50% in 2005.[8]

The drivers for firms adopting CSR practices vary by industry and by company. Companies may adopt CSR practices to realize public relations or marketing value. For instance, in one well-known example, Nike embraced CSR after a criticism of its overseas factory conditions hurt sales in the United States. Nike has since built a large CSR department and has led the apparel industry in developing and implementing rigorous supply chain CSR practices. Several companies in the apparel, footwear, oil and gas, chemical, toy, and consumer packaged goods industries have similarly incorporated CSR after major public crises or consumer boycotts.

Studies have also concluded that consumers state a preference for purchasing products from companies that employ CSR or corporate citizenship practices. (However, consumers' definitions of corporate citizenship vary widely, and their actual purchasing habits may not be correlated with their stated preference, indicating that consumer education is still needed.) Other firms see CSR as a differentiator in attracting the best talent in a competitive employment market. A study of "Millennial Generation" individuals (aged 13 to 25) concluded that 79% want to work for a company that cares about how it impacts or contributes to society.[9] Corporations may also see CSR as an avenue to decrease risks and liabilities, secure their basic license to operate, attract capital (e.g., socially responsible investing or social venture capital funds), decrease operating costs, or develop new customer markets.

Career search notes

In general, CSR is considered a cost center, so most full-time corporate CSR positions are at large companies. Smaller companies may incorporate CSR responsibilities into another executive function or department. Even at large companies, CSR departments tend to be small corporate groups that report to the legal affairs, public affairs, environment health & safety (EHS) directors, or, in some cases, directly to the CEO. They often hire from within the company and seldom recruit on campus, so getting an "in" typically requires persistence and determined networking — but is not impossible. In recent years, there have been significantly more advertised job openings for CSR professionals posted to job boards, as the field has grown. There are also emerging opportunities with specialized CSR consulting firms — some of which manage CSR compliance issues, while others focus on public relations or CSR reporting.

Some industries hire more CSR professionals than others. A 2008 survey by Ellen Weinreb and Net Impact found that, of advertised CSR job openings, nearly half of the corporate CSR positions were in either the apparel or the consumer packaged goods industry. Top employers included Nike, Starbucks, and The Walt Disney Company. Consulting firms, research institutes, and CSR membership associations like Business for Social Responsibility (USA) and Business in the Community (UK) are also leading employers for CSR professionals.

Example job titles include:

- Program Manager, Social and Environmental Accountability, Microsoft

- Compliance Manager, International Labor Standards Group, The Walt Disney Company

- Senior Consultant, Verité

- Global Compliance Analyst, Target

- Human Rights Manager, Phillips-Van Heusen

- Vice President, Corporate Social Responsibility, Fleishman-Hillard

- Corporate Responsibility Consultant, Sustainability and Environment, Business in the Community

Responsibilities in a typical CSR position might include:

- Issues and crisis management

- Government relations

- Community engagement and outreach

- Stakeholder management

- Regulatory relations

- Grassroots communications

- Safety and labor standards compliance

- Employee training

- Corporate citizenship or CSR reporting

- Coordinating employee volunteerism and community service activities

- Project management

While CSR strategy can be exciting, be prepared for a CSR position to also involve a high degree of compliance and reporting duties. This might include compiling corporate safety and labor statistics, auditing factories, conducting CSR training programs, or writing supplier purchasing policies. "Know what you're getting into," says Ellen Weinreb, founder of Sustainability Recruiting. "When you are accepting a job, think about what the tasks are that you're going to be doing day to day. Don't just look at the title." Some students get excited about the prospect of a CSR manager position but don't look closely enough at the job description to know what that really involves on a daily basis.

Employers are typically looking for candidates who have a solid understanding of the business case for corporate responsibility. It's important for your heart to be in the right place, but equally important to know how CSR can translate to the bottom line, and to be able to articulate that in a compelling way. "Most employers are looking for somebody who is passionate about CSR, but also demonstrates a strong understanding of the business," says Weinreb.

Prior corporate experience in a related industry is helpful. If you don't have that in your pre-MBA background, look for ways to create that experience during school (see "Gaining experience" on page 40 for ideas).

Tips

✓ Try to attend the BSR annual conference, whether you can get a position as a conference volunteer or you have to pay to attend. The registration fee is exorbitant (typically over $1,000), but the networking with CSR professionals is invaluable (And, yes, some MBA students *have* paid that fee to attend. And, yes, have made contacts at the conference that led directly to CSR job offers.)

Marcy Scott Lynn holds the enviable role of Director of Corporate Sustainability and Responsibility with Sun Microsystems, based in Santa Clara, California. She oversees Sun's non-financial reporting, as well as stakeholder and employee engagement around CSR and sustainability.

Though she loves her job and knows it is the perfect fit for her, she counsels students to think twice about a CSR department job. "For students who have some hard skills — finance, accounting, operations, or marketing — I believe strongly that if you take those hard skills and go into a business function job, you can have a lot more impact than in the CSR department."

Found her current position . . .

. . . by emailing a "cold" contact at Sun and requesting an informational interview. Within the first few minutes of the call, he told her about a new position that was about to be created.

Her job search tips

✓ Don't be shy. These jobs don't just fall in your lap; you've got to reach out and network

✓ You can't take "no" personally. Don't be upset if you email a contact and they don't email you back

✓ There's nothing like experience. Find ways to work on relevant real-world projects during school — independent studies, class projects, internships during the school year. You can practice being bold by calling a company up and saying, "I'd like to do a project for you. Here's what that would mean . . ."

Those determined to work in the CSR department need strong analytical, communication (written and verbal), and negotiating skills. Marcy started her career in politics, and then worked in crisis and issues management communications before business school. "My communications background was important because the biggest part of the job is communicating."

Like many others, Marcy says an independent study project during business school was critical to her job hunting success. As a first-year MBA student at the Haas School of Business at UC–Berkeley, she and two classmates worked on a project about socially responsible investing for Yahoo!. The project gave her real insights on CSR issues in the tech sector, and she leveraged that expertise in reaching out to other tech companies. After her summer internship, she did a second (part-time) internship during the school year with another tech company, Symantec. All of these experiences put her in the "right place at the right time" when she contacted Sun Micro-systems for an informational interview.

"I really feel like there are times when I am having a positive impact," she says. "I love that about my job."

✓ Consider joining a company in a traditional role (for instance, marketing) and positioning yourself to move into a CSR role — or integrate CSR into your role — after you have learned the business

✓ Understand where CSR sits in the organizational structure of the company you are applying for. For instance, is it a part of the legal department, communications department, government affairs, or a standalone function? The skills the company is looking for may be slanted based on how the CSR group is organized

✓ BSR has one of the best lists for CSR job postings (www.bsr.org). Lifeworth (www.lifeworth.com) has a free monthly CSR jobs e-bulletin. The "CSR-Jobs" Yahoo! group (http://finance.groups.yahoo.com/group/csr-jobs) is a useful source for primarily Europe-based CSR job openings

✓ Set up a CSR job search agent on meta-search sites like JustMeans.com or SimplyHired.com as an efficient way to find advertised openings

Corporate environmental management/corporate sustainability

Keywords

Corporate sustainability, climate change, triple bottom line, environmental management systems, sustainable development, Dow Jones Sustainability Index, sustainable supply chain, product stewardship, EHS

Example employers

Ford, DuPont, IBM, Citigroup, Alcoa, Hewlett-Packard, Weyerhaeuser, Boise Cascade, FedEx, Dow, UPS, BASF, ABB, BP, Intel, Timken, GE, Interface, AT&T, Bank of America, Citigroup, Home Depot, other large corporations

Areas of focus

Sustainability strategy; Environment, health, and safety (EHS) management and reporting; Environmental management systems (EMS)/ISO 14001; Risk management; Issues management; Stakeholder engagement

Skills needed

Quantitative analysis and modeling; Project management; Leading, motivating, and training personnel; Cost–benefit analysis; Business planning and budgeting; Change management; Communications and reporting; Strategy; Negotiations

Key resources

- Annual State of Green Business Report, www.stateofgreenbusiness.com
- ClimateBiz, www.climatebiz.com
- Corporate Eco Forum, www.corporateecoforum.com
- Dow Jones Sustainability Index, www.sustainability-index.com
- GreenBiz, www.greenbiz.com
- Global Reporting Initiative, www.globalreporting.org
- Net Impact, www.netimpact.org
- Sustainable Business job board, www.greendreamjobs.com
- Corporate EHS reports

Main issues

As discussed in other places in this guide, corporate sustainability is on the rise — as are jobs for MBAs in corporate sustainability or environmental management departments — though demand for these jobs still outpaces their availability.

Corporate environmental, health, and safety (EHS) departments are not new — particularly in industries with significant environmental or safety exposures (e.g., chemical, manufacturing, and mining industries). However, the integration of corporate environmental management with sustainability strategy and/or corporate social responsibility strategy is a relatively newer approach. We are also seeing a broader range of industries adopting corporate sustainability functions.

Corporate sustainability departments may incorporate responsibilities such as:

- Environmental impact assessment and monitoring

- Environmental management systems (EMS)

- Product stewardship/life-cycle analysis

- Climate change strategy

- Stakeholder engagement

- Employee training

- Environmental communication and reporting

Depending on the company and organizational structure, the corporate sustainability department may or may not be involved with the development of new products or services related to sustainability.

Career search notes

Like CSR departments, corporate sustainability/environmental departments tend to be small and viewed as cost centers for companies. For that reason, it can sometimes be hard to enter these departments directly.

Many (though not all) corporate environmental management positions have a technical component, so an MBA alone is sometimes not enough. Some employers look for individuals with a science or engineering undergraduate degree or an additional master's degree in a technical field like environmental management.

Example job titles include:

- Environmental Sustainability Program Manager, Xerox Corporation

- Director, Partnerships & Communications, Worldwide EHS, Johnson & Johnson

- Manager, Emerging Technologies & Climate Change, Puget Sound Energy

- Corporate Sustainable Development Consultant, Procter & Gamble

- Sustainable Development Assistant Summer Intern, Bayer

Corporate sustainability initiatives often involve investment in equipment or changes to corporate policies, but many also require extensive efforts to change employee behavior. For instance, a company may seek to reduce its energy usage by encouraging employees to turn off computers at the end of each day. Because of this, sustainability manager positions nearly always require strong skills in change management strategies, employee training, and stakeholder communications.

Lindsay James pursued her MBA with a career in sustainability as her goal, but she wanted to broaden her business perspective first. So, after graduating with her MBA from UNC's Kenan-Flagler Business School, she took a position with an economic consulting firm in Dallas, Texas. Consulting was invaluable for building Lindsay's skills in project and client management, and after two years she was ready to re-position herself and focus on sustainability in a strategic corporate or consulting role.

She was excited when she saw an opening with the corporate sustainability group at Interface. Heralded as an early sustainable business leader in the influential book *Natural*

Found her current position . . .

. . . when several colleagues forwarded a circulating job opening. An MBA classmate who knew the hiring manager sent a personal recommendation that got Lindsay a first-round interview; detailed research and preparation got her through three rounds of interviews and a final presentation to the decision-makers.

Her job search tips

✓ Really know your strengths and be able to communicate them. What is your competitive advantage? You can use a tool like Gallup's StrengthsFinder, or others to help you identify your strengths

✓ Come up with your own definition of sustainability. Be able to answer the question of "what is sustainability?" in your own words in a meaningful way

✓ Having any formal education in sustainability is a real differentiator; if you have taken sustainability courses in business school, recognize and promote the value of that

Capitalism,[10] the carpet manufacturer Interface has made a concerted effort to stay at the forefront of sustainability practices.

> ✓ Greenbiz.com, Grist.org, and Joel Makower's blog are good sources for news. If you know what industry you're going into, look for important industry-specific publications

To stand out in the interview process, Lindsay undertook extensive research and preparation. "I created a comprehensive binder on Interface with everything I could find. I read the past five years' annual reports, read all the cases on the website, read industry news (carpet manufacturing and green building), and did informational interviews with every Interface connection I could find. I even stopped by the local Interface showroom to see the product and talk to the showroom manager. When I finally got to the interview, I could engage in a strategic conversation and highlight my understanding of the industry challenges and opportunities." Her preparation showed her passion as well as her solid foundation in sustainability strategy. "Passion goes a long way with values-based organizations," she says. "They want to see that you share the company's values — but you must also present a keen understanding of the market forces."

In her role as director of strategic sustainability at Interface in Chicago, Lindsay's main goal is to leverage Interface's sustainability leadership to enhance the company's competitive advantage. She undertakes competitive positioning, strategy, stakeholder management, sales force training, and client outreach and education. Lindsay underscores the importance of professional development in her role: "To maintain expertise in such a rapidly changing field like sustainability requires a strong commitment to learning."

While MBAs are often excited about the strategy aspects of these positions, note that these positions often include environmental compliance, monitoring, reporting, and employee training functions.

Tips

✓ Be sure to read the EHS reports of any companies of interest, along with those of their industry peers/competitors

✓ If you are interested in a particular industry (e.g., pharmaceutical, consumer packaged goods, or automobile manufacturing), participate in industry association events to build your network

✓ Consider joining a company in a traditional role (e.g., marketing) and positioning yourself to move into a corporate sustainability role after you have learned the business

✓ Try to understand the whole spectrum of environmental issues applicable to the company or industry; issues might include not only regulatory compliance issues but also corporate operational footprint, raw materials sourcing, product life-cycle issues, and climate change risk, among others

✓ Greendreamjobs.com and Net Impact's job board are two great resources for corporate environmental and sustainability job openings

Sustainability consulting

Keywords

Sustainability consulting, triple bottom line, sustainability/CSR reporting, strategy

Example employers

SustainAbility, GreenOrder, KPMG, Deloitte, PricewaterhouseCoopers, DOMANI, Sustainable Value Partners, Blu Skye Consulting, Rocky Mountain Institute, Five Winds International, Eco-Nomics, AccountAbility, Ecos Corporation, Origo, ARUP, The Natural Step, Kinetix LLC, Sustainability Institute, ICF International, Natural Logic, Framework: CR

Areas of focus

Sustainability strategy, benchmarking, and best practices; Supply chain sustainability analysis; Organizational change strategy; Strategic communications; Metrics and measurement

Skills needed

Corporate strategy and industry analysis tools; Management consulting frameworks; Client management; Project management; Business planning

Key resources

- Esty, D.C., and A.S. Winston, *Green to Gold: How Smart Companies Use Environmental Strategy to Innovate, Create Value, and Build Competitive Advantage* (Yale University Press, 2006)
- GreenBiz, www.greenbiz.com
- Laszlo, C., *Sustainable Value: How the World's Leading Companies Are Doing Well by Doing Good* (Greenleaf Publishing, 2008)
- Joel Makower's blog, http://makower.typepad.com
- SustainAbility, www.sustainability.com
- World Business Council for Sustainable Development, www.wbcsd.org

Main issues

As sustainability has gained traction as a mainstream business idea, demand has grown for consulting services that focus specifically on sustainability strategy, marketing, and reporting. In response, sustainability consulting as an industry has been growing rapidly in recent years. This growth has slowed somewhat during the recent economic recession in the USA, but there is still demand for consulting services in many industries, particularly among companies that see sustainability as a path to eco-efficiency or other cost savings.

The definition, quality, and scope of services offered by sustainability consulting firms vary widely. Some firms focus on the strategic business aspects of sustainability, while others are more technical — for instance, energy auditing or greenhouse gas emissions modeling. There are even firms that focus exclusively on sustainability reporting.

In general, sustainable business consulting services often include:

- Sustainability strategy assessment, recommendations, and implementation

- Sustainability/CSR/non-financial reporting guidance and auditing

- Stakeholder relations, stakeholder engagement strategies

- Management of supply chain environmental or CSR issues

- Product design and life-cycle analysis related to CSR and environmental issues

- Organizational change strategy

Firms take different angles on the topics and have differing methodologies for the work, so there are many services beyond these.

Career search notes

Until recently, sustainability consulting was a niche field of small players and was very difficult to enter. Now, many sustainability firms are hiring regularly (some even recruiting on campus), and large firms like Deloitte and KPMG are adding sustainability and CSR services. This is still a small and competitive field, but the opportunities are growing.

Jeff Gowdy (MBA 2006), founder of J. Gowdy Consulting, advises, "Understand where you want to fit into the consulting realm. I break it out into three parts: (1) upfront strategic planning/strategy development; (2) implementation and project management; and (3) marketing and communications. You can focus on one or more but really need to develop the skills in an area to have the expertise before consulting." He also emphasizes, "The environmental knowledge is the real wildcard for MBAs. You must understand the ecological aspects of the work in order to provide real consulting value to clients."

Firms that call themselves sustainability consultants can range from established strategists working with major corporations to one-person outfits doing energy audits for local businesses. Because the focus and credentials can vary so much, it is important to research any firms you are considering joining, especially small or new ones. You might talk to some of their current and past employees, ask to see example project deliverables from recent projects, and/or talk to some of their clients. A firm may show you an impressive client list, but may not have as much business rigor behind that work as you'd like.

It is also important that you have a strong rapport with, and respect for, the firm's founding partners and associates that you'll be working with. This is true of any small or entrepreneurial company, but perhaps more important in a consulting practice where you can expect to be working in teams nearly all of the time and are hoping to be trained in a new body of knowledge about the practice of sustainability from the partners.

After graduating from the Kellogg School of Management at Northwestern University, Marc Major wanted to pursue a career that let him apply business thinking to address social issues. He had considered management consulting as a career but rejected it because, he says, "When I got out of business school, I felt a little too old to do something I didn't really care about. Regular consulting would have been a great challenge, but I knew that if I didn't feel moved by the purpose behind it all, I would never last doing it."

When an opportunity came up to work on a short-term project with Sustainable Value Partners, however, it seemed an ideal combination of challenge and social purpose, so Marc took it. That project turned into full-time sustainability consulting work with SVP and another firm, Blu Skye. He was

Found his first sustainability consulting position . . .

. . . through networking, and being flexible. When Sustainable Value Partners had a short-term consulting project need, Marc heard about it through word of mouth in his network, applied, and was hired on a temporary contract basis.

His job search tips

✓ Real-world experience is a must
✓ Don't become a consultant just because you don't know what else to do. This has to be what you want to do *above all else*
✓ Sustainability consulting companies are very specific in what they want; they each have a different approach and philosophy. It's about fit. So, if you don't get a job with one firm, it doesn't mean that you won't be a great fit with another

lucky to join right as the firm was signing up a project to help Wal-Mart develop its sustainability agenda.

The most fulfilling part of that work for Marc was the chance to work with such an influential company on sustainability strategy. He knew that Wal-Mart's decisions could affect entire supply chains. "We were able to help a lot of people who had never given these issues much thought to see the importance and business opportunity inherent in environmental and social sustainability . . . There was this moment when stakeholder pressure and world events and resource constraints aligned into the perfect storm. It created a window to bring in some very influential thinkers and help the company try on a new mindset — a new way of thinking about the future of the business."

In his role as consultant, Marc helps companies weave sustainability into their business strategies and long-term planning processes, and execute those strategies in a way that adds long-term value to both shareholders and stakeholders. Now co-founder of a new consultancy, Cleargreen Advisors, Marc looks for MBAs who are "sharp, flexible, rigorous, and interesting in a way that is different" when he hires consultants.

One piece of advice he offers: "Don't try to become the sustainability specialist in a company. Most companies don't have many of those and frequently the ones they do have enjoy little real power. Be the person you already are — performing the function you're already passionate about — and add sustainability to that. One of my mentors in this business taught me that if sustainability is going to be successful, it can't be bolted on. It has to be integrated, and woven throughout the business."

Example job titles include:

- Strategist, Kinetix LLC

- Managing Consultant, Blu Skye

- Senior Consultant, Energy & Resources Team, Rocky Mountain Institute

- Consultant, Sustainable Value Partners

- Analyst, Rocky Mountain Institute

- Business Development Manager, Saatchi & Saatchi S

As with any management consulting position, the lifestyle of a sustainability consultant can be taxing. The workload is rigorous and may require travel as much as 80 or 100% of the time, depending on the projects you're working on. Another challenge is that you're never really an expert in your client's business, and you may meet with a high degree of skepticism about the sustainability agenda from employees on-site. Because of this, successful sustainability consultants are not only knowledgeable but also likeable and persuasive. "As with any consulting engagement, you've sometimes got to convince the client of things they'd rather not see or admit. This requires building a relationship, and the more personable you are, the stronger the bonds you can build," says sustainability consultant Marc Major (MBA 2004). "If you can form brilliant, persuasive arguments but are someone no one can stand to be around, your bright ideas are going to hit a brick wall."

The most important step in landing a position in sustainability consulting is networking. This is true whether you are targeting small companies or large ones. Even at large firms like Deloitte, the sustainability group is relatively small, so you need to be on the radar of the associates working specifically within that initiative. At small firms, hiring is typically done on a quick-turnaround, as-needed basis — often on personal referrals. Open positions will probably not be advertised on campus, and may not even be posted online. If you are in touch with the partners, you will be more likely to be considered when an opening arises.

Tips

✓ Network through any, and all, possible channels. Develop relationships with partners in the firms that interest you most. Try to meet them at conferences or other events. Invite them to your campus as speakers or competition judges

✓ Many small firms hire consultants for intermittent contract work before a full-time position is available. When talking with firms, ask if there are opportunities to work with them on projects part-time (for either pay or academic credit) during the school year to get your foot in the door. Once you have demonstrated your capabilities on a project, you will be a natural fit for any full-time job openings or continued contract work with the firm

✓ You will need to excel at both MBA fundamentals (marketing, finance, operations) *and* sustainability. Neither is enough on its own. Be sure you have a strong portfolio of sustainability experiences to discuss in interviews — whether class projects, an independent study, or extracurricular activities. Demonstrated commitment to sustainability and an entrepreneurial spirit are usually critical. A consulting concentration and / or management consulting experience is also helpful

Green building/
sustainable real estate development

Keywords

Green building, affordable housing, sustainable community planning, brownfield remediation, urban redevelopment, LEED, smart growth

Example employers

Centex Homes, Kinetix LLC, Cherokee Investment Partners, Elm Street Development, Bank of America Corporate Workplace Group, Enterprise Community Group, GE Real Estate

Areas of focus

Green building project development and finance; Property management; Asset management

Skills needed

Project management; Budgeting/proformas; Financial analysis; Business planning; Cost–benefit analysis; Purchasing

Key resources

- National Brownfield Associations, www.brownfieldassociation.org
- Smart Growth America, www.smartgrowthamerica.org
- Urban Land Institute, www.uli.org
- US Green Building Council, www.usgbc.org

Main issues

"Green building" — sometimes also called "high-performance building" — refers to the practice of reducing the environmental impact of the built environment. Few applications of sustainability have attracted as much attention in recent years as green building, particularly in the commercial real estate sector.

Amid the real estate industry financial crisis, green building projects have suffered along with the rest of the industry. Still, green building retains promise — especially among government and military projects, many of which are required to meet certain green building standards. According to McGraw-Hill's *2009 Green Outlook Report*, green building construction totaled only $10 billion in 2005 but is projected to increase to between $96 and $140 billion by 2013.

"There are two trends that we saw happening before the recession that will be further developed," says Marc Heisterkamp (MBA 2007), Director of Commercial Real Estate for the US Green Building Council. "We'll see more green building in government buildings in general; a lot of federal money is going there, and the markets are more insulated than speculative development. The other trend we see is a shift towards retrofitting existing buildings. Because everyone's looking to cut operating costs, and green building is a way to do that, we see a fair amount of growth opportunities in retrofit projects."

Green buildings are typically more energy- and water-efficient; they use environmentally preferable materials, siting, construction techniques, and operational practices. An important standard is the LEED (Leadership in Energy and Environmental Design) certification system developed by the US Green Building Council.

Green buildings return value to their owners in several ways. The link to energy prices is apparent (green buildings are often significantly more energy-efficient than their counterparts) but, interestingly, the biggest bang-for-the-buck often comes from human factors:

- Workforce productivity improvements

- Employee attraction and retention results

Several studies have shown that workers are more productive and have lower absentee rates in green buildings.[11] In addition, companies competing for talent, like Bank of America, have found attractive green building space to be a draw for employees; Bank of America designed its new corporate headquarters building in New York City to be the first LEED Platinum-certified building in the city.

Career search notes

Until the real estate crisis began in 2008, jobs for MBAs in green building were growing steadily. While it is hard to predict when and how the industry will recover, it is likely that, when it does, green building will be an important focus. With energy efficiency a key theme of both the Obama Administration and the American Recovery and Reinvestment Act of 2009, it is likely that green building will only become more important. Furthermore, many government, military, and institutional agencies now have policies that mandate that any new construction meets LEED or ENERGY STAR standards.

In general, careers for MBAs in green building may include project management, market analysis, finance, or business development for real estate developers, construction companies, financiers, real estate investment trusts (REITs), or building product manufacturers and distributors. There are also firms that specialize in green building consulting which hire MBAs (examples include Kinetix LLC, DOMANI, and Paladino). These consulting firms tend to be small and hire only intermittently, so networking is key. Other sustainability-related careers in the real estate arena include affordable housing development, community development finance, and urban planning and redevelopment. There are career paths for MBAs in all these areas.

Example green building job titles include:

- Manager, Commercial Real Estate, US Green Building Council

- Senior Vice President, Corporate Workplace, Bank of America

- Director, Real Estate and Facilities Lending, Self-Help Credit Union

- Green Building Consultant, Senior Analyst, The Green Roundtable, Inc.

- Director of Property Operations & Engineering, Corporate Office Properties Trust

One way to differentiate yourself is to become either a LEED Accredited Professional or a LEED Green Associate by taking and passing an exam with the US Green Building Council to demonstrate proficiency in green building practices. Accreditation is increasingly recognized as vital to successful involvement in a green project, regardless of role. Also, note that few companies are looking to hire solely green building specialists but require that such skills be coupled with more conventional skills in marketing, operations, finance, and project management. Conventional real estate experience, combined with green building interests, is important to most employers. A dual MBA/Masters of Regional Planning (MRP) may be helpful if you wish to focus on the land use aspects of sustainable development, but is not necessary for most green building roles.

Finally, another option to consider in the midst of the real estate industry's downturn is renewable energy project develop-

Annie Lux never thought she would be working for a big production home-builder. As a student in the dual degree MBA/Masters of Regional Planning program at the University of North Carolina, her entire focus was on advancing the green building agenda. She knew she wanted to work somewhere that was progressive on the issue.

When Centex came to recruit on campus, she interviewed for a strategic marketing internship with them as "an experiment." She was surprised that Centex not only valued her green building perspective but also had a green project for her to work on. She spent her summer doing market research on consumer attitudes towards green homes.

Found her current position . . .

. . . through a traditional on-campus recruiting interview and internship.

Her job search tips

✓ You have to be more flexible than in the past. You have to be willing to do almost anything in the industry

✓ It helps to get your LEED certification while you're in school, while the cost is low and you have (relatively) more time to study

✓ The Urban Land Institute (ULI) is the best networking avenue for anyone interested in development. Anybody who's anybody in real estate is involved with ULI — bankers, developers, consulting firms, they are all in ULI

✓ Work with a company during school, even if you're not paid. The best job advice I ever got was "start doing something for free and eventually they have to pay you"

She ended up liking not only the project, but also the company culture, and accepted a full-time offer with Centex in Raleigh, North Carolina. Now a marketing manager with the company, she has a traditional marketing role, but finds ways to integrate her green building interests into her job, like marketing the "Centex Energy Advantage" home program. "If you want to be effective in a company, you can't be seen as myopic and only focused on 'green,' " she says. "If you want to be able to move around the organization, you have to be able to be part of everything else too."

When asked if Centex will likely scale back its focus on green building because of the recession, Annie says, "Definitely not. We figured out how to add all these great features to our houses at minimal cost. Consumers love it. It's a quality advantage as much as a cost savings issue with consumers."

The real estate industry downturn has made jobs hard to come by, but increased the focus on green building. "It actually helps you now if you are interested in green building, because it's the newest, hottest thing in the real estate industry," Annie says. While development and finance jobs are scarce, her advice to MBA job seekers interested in this field is: "Try to get a job anywhere in real estate — sales, marketing, consulting — and then carve out your niche."

"Learn as much as you can, so you're an expert before you come out of school, and have some legitimacy right away." She adds, "But then, be flexible. The field is always changing."

ment. A role as project developer for a large solar or wind energy development requires many of the same skills as large-scale commercial real estate development. For example, see the category of "Property & Real Estate" openings on the job board at www. RenewableEnergyWorld.com. Major electric utility companies have also been hiring real estate professionals to manage their energy efficiency initiatives and programs, so you could look into the utility sector as well.

Tips

✓ Follow the changing regulations and incentives that are creating green building standards around the country

✓ Understand the financial benefits of green building and be able to identify some of the low-hanging fruit of resource-efficient buildings

✓ Join the Urban Land Institute (ULI) and the US Green Building Council (USGBC) and participate in events arranged by your local chapters. Both these organizations have chapters for students and young professionals (ULI's "Young Leaders Groups" and USGBC's "Emerging Green Builders"). You can also create job alerts on both organizations' Career Center web pages to email you new job openings automatically

✓ The annual Greenbuild conference and expo (www. greenbuildexpo.org) is the biggest industry event (nearly 30,000 attendees in 2008) and an excellent networking opportunity. The Urban Land Institute also hosts an annual green building conference which focuses more heavily on real estate development and finance aspects (www.uli.org/Events/Events.aspx)

Renewable energy industry jobs

Keywords

Wind energy, solar energy, biofuels/biomass, alternative energy, ethanol, fuel cells, clean energy, cleantech

Example employers

Green Mountain Energy, GE Energy, Vestas, Airtricity, BP Solar, SkyPower, SunPower, Ballard Power, Solargenix, SunEdison; developers, equipment manufacturers, clean energy venture capitalists, green power utilities, renewable energy think tanks or policy institutes

Areas of focus

Wind or solar project development; Business development and sales; Strategic marketing; Cleantech venture capital/finance; Technology commercialization

Skills needed

Financial analysis and budgeting; Project management; Strategic market and competitive analysis; Business-to-business sales; Business planning; Operations; Community and government relations

Key resources

- American Solar Energy Society, www.ases.org
- American Wind Energy Association, www.awea.org
- Canadian Solar Industries Association, www.cansia.ca
- Canadian Wind Energy Association, www.canwea.ca
- Energy Information Administration's Renewable Energy Basics, www.eia.doe.gov/basics/renewalt_basics.html
- Greenjobs.com, www.greenjobs.com
- Greentech Media, www.greentechmedia.com →

- National Renewable Energy Lab, www.nrel.gov
- REN21 (Renewable Energy Policy Network for the 21st Century), www.ren21.net
- Renewable Energy World, www.renewableenergyworld.com
- Solar Buzz, www.solarbuzz.com
- Solar Energy Industries Association, www.seia.org
- US Department of Energy, Office of Energy Efficiency & Renewable Energy, www.eere.energy.gov

Main issues

Renewable energy is energy derived from naturally replenishing sources such as solar, wind, biomass, water (hydroelectric), and geothermal sources, though most often when speaking about the renewable energy industry, the context refers to wind or solar (photovoltaic) electric power generation.

According to the *2007 Global Status Report* by REN21 (Renewable Energy Policy Network for the 21st Century), "renewable electricity generation capacity reached an estimated 240 gigawatts (GW) worldwide in 2007, an increase of 50% over 2004." This is a tiny fraction of the world's energy consumption (3.4%), but it is growing, and the increasing rate of investment in large-scale wind and solar developments signals that renewables will make up a larger percentage of total world energy generating capacity and consumption in the future.

Right now, renewable energy costs more to generate per kilowatt hour than nuclear, coal, or natural gas generation. That is improving, though, as renewable energy technologies become more efficient, demand drives economies of scale, and government policies incentivize renewables. The adoption of a carbon tax or carbon cap-and-trade system will also make renewable energy more cost-competitive because renewables typically emit no carbon dioxide, whereas energy derived from fossil fuels has a large carbon footprint.

The clean energy space is evolving so quickly it is difficult to summarize all the key issues and trends in just a few paragraphs. There are several clean energy primers and market outlook reports available online. Books on energy sustainability abound, and range from the more straightforward (renewable energy handbooks and policy guides) to the more provocative (*The End of Oil, The Prize, The Hydrogen Economy,* or *Hubbert's Peak*[12]). There are also career guides devoted specifically to renewable energy industry jobs.

MBAs interested in the topic should understand what is meant by terms like "peak oil," "feed-in tariffs," "distributed generation," "renewable portfolio standards (RPSs or REPSs)," and "renewable energy credits (RECs)." You should also understand the drivers for renewable energy adoption, and develop a basic understanding of the different technologies and their limitations, applications, and cost–benefit profiles.

Other clean energy sectors that are distinct from renewable energy but may also be of interest include:

- Energy efficiency technologies

- Alternative fuels (e.g., biomass, ethanol, and hydrogen)

- "Smart grid" technologies

Career search notes

There are several different types of players in the renewable energy industry including:

- Developers

- Equipment manufacturers

- Generating utilities

- Financiers (cleantech venture capital, REC traders)

- Policy-makers

With renewable energy developers like Iberdrola Renewables, SunEdison, SkyPower, NextEra Energy Resources or Horizon, the two most likely career avenues for MBAs are through finance or development. Manufacturers of photovoltaic and wind energy technologies (such as GE, Vestas, Gamesa, or Sharp) also hire MBAs. For example, GE has an MBA rotational program called the Renewable Energy Leadership Program, which hires both interns and full-time professionals.

Because the technologies and issues are highly technical, manufacturers and developers often look for candidates who have an engineering background in addition to an MBA. If you don't have a technical background, you would be well served to spend some time learning about the details of different technologies and understanding the industry context and technology trends. "You have to show that you have done everything possible to learn about the industry, so that you won't start at ground zero," says Natacha Kiler (MBA 2007), Marketing Services Manager for SunEdison.

Most of the big oil and gas companies have renewable energy development divisions, but rarely recruit MBAs directly into those divisions. According to one recruiter at Shell, MBAs typically enter the company through the management rotational program and have to be prepared to work in any division of the company — whether that is in renewable energy or in exploration and production.

Another opportunity for MBAs to add value is in technology commercialization for emerging energy technologies. This could be at a government lab like Los Alamos National Laboratory or the National Renewable Energy Laboratory (NREL), or at a clean energy business incubator (see the National Alliance of Clean Energy Incubators for ideas). MBAs with a public policy background may find different opportunities with government agencies, industry associations, or think tanks like the Renewable Energy Policy Project (REPP).

Some example job titles include:

- Senior Financial Analyst, Green Mountain Energy

- Renewables Director, International Power

- Director of Product Marketing, Utilities, SunEdison

- Renewable Energy Project Analyst, Lawrence Berkeley National Laboratory

- Strategic Business Management, Wind Energy, Siemens Power Generation

- Intern, Renewable Energy Leadership Program, GE

- Biofuels Specialist, Novozymes North America

- Energy Finance Development Manager, Vermont Energy Investment Corporation

Tips

✓ Industry conferences are great places not only to network, but also to get up to speed on the latest technology and policy developments facing the industry. Several notable examples are WINDPOWER (the American Wind Energy Association's annual conference and expo), Solar Power International, Intersolar North America, RETECH, and EnergyWorld North America. You can find others through a quick Google search or on events calendars with industry groups like the Solar Energy Industries Association. There are dozens of state and regional events on renewable energy and sustainable energy annually, as well

When Michelle Chislett started as an MBA student at the Schulich School of Business at York University in Toronto, she knew she was ready for a career change from the telecommunications industry, but she wasn't sure exactly what she wanted to do after graduation. "I spent a lot of time in my first semester speaking to a variety of people in a variety of fields," she recounts. "I really liked the people I talked to in the renewable energy sector. They were really passionate about their jobs. I caught the bug."

Renewable energy companies were not among the on-campus recruiters at York at the time, so Michelle attended lots of industry conferences. At one event, she connected

Found her current position . . .

. . . after an informational interview led to a job offer.

Her job search tips

✓ Candidates need to be able to understand both the business case and the technical case for renewable energy. Having an engineering background can be an advantage, though it isn't necessarily a requirement

✓ Keep yourself well informed on the latest industry news by attending conferences and seminars

✓ One thing that can make you stand out is being up to speed on the latest government policies and incentives. These might be local, regional, or federal

✓ Volunteer with companies, with industry events, and with non-profits

✓ Regardless of your age and stage of life, one of the most helpful things to have during a career transition is a mentor that under-

with a wind energy developer and offered to work for them as a volunteer during her second year of the MBA program. Months later, when she had an informational interview with the CEO of Sky-Power, she had real-world experience in the renewable energy industry to draw on; he offered her a position the same week.

stands you personally as well as professionally

✓ Several Canadian renewable energy companies are expanding into the USA and opening satellite offices. US-based MBAs may find opportunities with them

SkyPower is a Canadian-based renewable energy developer that manages wind and solar projects from initial site exploration through resource assessment, financing, permitting, and construction. Now the vice president of SkyPower's Solar Project Development Group, Michelle oversees business development, project development, and community relations for the company's solar projects. "I use a wide variety of skills in my job," she says. "No two days are the same. One day I'm out in the field in my boots, making sure that a project is going well, and the next day, I'm in an office talking to the bank."

Michelle credits her own job search success to her volunteer experience, and advises others to do the same. "The biggest disadvantage candidates have today is that everyone is interested in sustainability, but very few people actually have experience in it." She urges students to find a way to build some industry expertise, whether through an internship or school project. She also looks for candidates who are dynamic, accustomed to change, and flexible in an industry that is changing every day. "I need people who are dedicated to this field," she says. "Their passion is the best thing they have going for them."

✓ Get up to speed on the latest developments in legislation and tax incentives. New government policies will have huge impacts on industry dynamics and drivers

✓ As with other sustainability careers, relevant industry experience is critical. Try to gain experience by working directly with a renewable energy company through a class project or practicum project

✓ There are several career search websites and recruiting agencies devoted specifically to careers in the energy sector. See the list of job posting websites on page 143 for some ideas, but there are also new ones emerging every day

Socially responsible investing (SRI)

Keywords

SRI, ESG investment analysis, double- or triple-bottom-line investing, sustainability index, finance, responsible investment, sustainable finance

Example employers

Calvert, Sustainable Asset Management, KLD Research & Analytics, Trillium Asset Management, Generation Investment Management, Riskmetrics, Innovest, Domini Social Investments, EIRIS, Robeco, Henderson Global Investors, Deutsche Bank Asset Management

Areas of focus

Investment research and analysis, finance, money management, marketing

Skills needed

Strong quantitative and qualitative analysis tools; Financial analysis and modeling; Industry expertise; Client management; Marketing the sustainable investment case

Key resources

- Dow Jones Sustainability Indexes, www.sustainability-index.com
- Environmental Finance, www.environmental-finance.com
- SocialFunds, www.socialfunds.com
- Social Investment Forum, www.socialinvest.org including *2007 Report on Socially Responsible Investing Trends in the United States*, www.socialinvest.org/resources/research
- Responsible Investor, www.responsible-investor.com
- SRI in the Rockies, www.sriintherockies.com
- UN's Principles for Responsible Investment, www.unpri.org
- WSJ Environmental Capital blog, http://blogs.wsj.com/environmentalcapital

Main issues

Socially responsible investing (SRI) — sometimes also called sustainable investing or ethical investing — refers to investment strategies that seek to maximize financial return while maximizing social good and minimizing environmental footprint. While the term corporate social responsibility (CSR) has historically been used to explore extra-financial issues, "environmental–social–governance" (ESG) is currently the most common industry term to reference the factors integrated into investment analysis.

There are different approaches to SRI but, in general, socially responsible investors favor investments that:

- Promote environmental stewardship, consumer protection, human rights, removal of corruption, and diversity

- Avoid investments in certain industries that have negative social or environmental impacts

SRI may refer to the investment philosophy (how stocks, bonds, or assets are selected in practice) or to the process of engaging the companies invested in.

The first SRI mutual fund, the Pax World Balanced Fund, was launched in 1971 in the USA. By 2009, over 150 investment funds had been launched in the USA, offering a wide range of SRI investment criteria. According to the Social Investment Forum's *2007 Report on Socially Responsible Investing Trends in the USA*,[13] $2.7 trillion (or 11% of assets under professional management in the USA) were categorized as SRI in 2007, and the SRI category was growing at a faster pace than the broader universe of all investment assets under professional management. In the wake of the 2008 financial meltdown, many industry experts expect that SRI will continue to grow as investors demand greater responsibility and accountability.

There are different SRI investment methodologies. Some funds employ exclusionary screening, others focus on "best in class" strategies or shareholder advocacy. These methodologies have evolved over time, and have regional differences around the world. Asset owners, money managers, financial advisors, and investment service providers take different approaches to SRI, and often combine more than one strategy. There are also SRI index funds like the Domini 400 Social Index, the FTSE4Good Indexes, and the Dow Jones Sustainability Indexes. As well as understanding traditional investment banking and asset management terminology, a professional interested in SRI should be familiar with the basics of each of these different investment methodologies and regional differences.

ESG investment analysis may be used by either SRI investors or traditional investors to:

- Understand how a company's exposure to environmental, social, and governance risks and opportunities should be priced into asset valuation

- Assess the prospects for a company going forward

- Analyze the fundamental value of opportunities and risks faced by the firm

Career search notes

SRI career paths are similar to other investment banking paths, with options to work in company research, marketing/sales, or portfolio management. Examples include:

- Senior research analyst or research director with an SRI research house (e.g., Innovest, KLD Research & Analytics, Sustainable Asset Management, EIRIS)

- Product manager or marketing and sales team member with an SRI mutual fund (e.g., Calvert Funds, Pax World Funds, Domini Social Funds)

- Member of an ESG group at a traditional investment bank or index vendor (e.g., Goldman Sachs ESG Research Team, S&P US Carbon Efficient Index)

- Corporate governance policy advisor (pension fund or mutual fund) developing and executing the proxy voting policy across a firm's investment holdings (e.g., Legg Mason Proxy Advisory Unit)

Some other new opportunities that are arising in the SRI space are opportunities to work with pension funds or other institutional investors that are managing their own money and incorporating specific social or environmental criteria in new asset classes like sustainable forestry and water infrastructure, and new regions such as frontier markets like Mozambique, Costa Rica, and Vietnam. Many pension funds and rating agencies hire corporate governance specialists where the demand attracts revenue from paying clients. A 2009 report published by Robeco and Booz & Company projects the responsible investing market to become mainstream within asset management by 2015, reaching 15–20% of total global assets under management.[14]

Regardless of which career path you take, you'll be expected to have strong investment credentials (either pre-MBA or during school). Investment is a hyper-competitive field, so a robust understanding, sharp intellect, and ability to speak the language of investment banking are critical. Offering new and original ideas based on the data is one way to stand out. There is a lot of room to differentiate yourself on different environmental, social, or governance angles, either in the actual underlying research or its application in portfolio management.

SRI investors are continually inventing new ways to measure and monetize ESG impacts, opportunities and risks. One way to stand out is to bring some new ideas for metrics, measurement, or analysis to the conversation. This could be relevant to a particular industry (e.g., insights about community engagement issues as they relate to the big-box retail industry) or expertise in a particular environmental or social investment opportunity (e.g., carbon trading and carbon credits under the European Union Emissions Trading Scheme).

Example titles include:

- Responsible Investment Analyst, Mercer Investment Consulting

- Associate Index Manager, KLD Research & Analytics

- Socially Responsible Investing Analyst, ABN AMRO

- SRI Analyst, Pension Protection Fund, UK

- Analyst, Socially Responsible Investments, UBS

- Principal, ESG Investments, State Street Global Advisors

Tips

✓ Attend the annual "SRI in the Rockies" conference if you can; it's one of the best networking opportunities you'll have in the SRI space

✓ Be current on the very latest industry news. Responsible Investor (www.responsible-investor.com), SocialFunds. com (www.socialfunds.com), and Environmental Finance (www.environmental-finance.com) are three good sources, along with the requisite Wall Street Journal. For unusual insights, track blogs like Financial Advisor Green Blog

In 1995 Graham Sinclair was working as a pensions consultant in his native South Africa when he attended an investment presentation pitching both financial returns and social benefits in post-apartheid South Africa. He was inspired by the potential to manage investments in a way that simultaneously created investor returns and community development.

After several years of working in investment banking and global investment, Graham attended the MBA program at Villanova University with the goal of focusing on socially responsible investing. Working with a professor, he developed an independent study project on the drivers for SRI among US

Found his first SRI position . . .

. . . by doing an independent study project on SRI as an MBA student and building an SRI equity fund. These projects opened doors for interviews, and gave him the opportunity to present at industry conferences.

His job search tips

✓ Dream big. Don't be afraid to start your own investment fund. Or, go to a money manager and pitch them an entirely new idea

✓ Pitch hard at mutual fund companies that haven't yet grasped ESG issues, or haven't fully integrated them into their investment analyses

✓ Look at large international non-governmental organizations (NGOs), anyone with an endowment. How are they managing their money? Is it in line with their values? You could take your skills there

institutional investors. With another professor, he launched a live equity portfolio with an SRI mandate. The projects not only gave him an exceptional opportunity for networking

✓ Develop original ideas integrating ESG factors into the investment case, and pitch the ideas to asset owners and multilateral financing institutions with a mandate in the sustainability space

in the SRI industry, but also allowed him to develop some original insights which added value to industry professionals. He was invited to present at a major institutional investor conference, the IMN Green Mountain Summit. The paper and the conference opened doors for Graham that he might never have accessed otherwise.

After graduation, Graham joined KLD Research & Analytics (one of the stakeholders in his research). He spent two years at KLD before launching his own investment advisory boutique, Sinclair & Company LLC, consulting with institutional investors on the integration of ESG factors into investment practice. His consulting work has included working with institutional investors, and he led the UN Principles for Responsible Investment in Emerging Markets Project for the UNEP Finance Initiative through 2008.

Graham prefers the term "ESG Investment Architect" to explain his role in integrating sustainability and investment. "I don't actually manage people's money, but I develop the blueprint for how we will manage it. This is especially challenging on the frontiers of emerging markets investment."

As an employer now, Graham looks for clarity of vision, professionalism, and ESG insights, built upon a sharp MBA toolkit, in the candidates he interviews. "With any investment professional, if you are paying a premium for talent, you are expecting them to arrive in the morning every day with fresh ideas."

(www.fa-mag.com/green/blog/dorothy-hinchcliff.html) and SRI-Extra (http://sri-extra.blogspot.com)

✓ Social Investment Forum posts SRI industry jobs in the USA on its website (www.socialinvest.org/resources/ jobs), and EuroSIF covers Europe (www.eurosif.org/sri/ jobs)

✓ Participate in on-campus recruiting with traditional investment banks and use your knowledge of sustainability as a differentiator. Always bring it back to the bottom line:

- How do environmental, social or governance factors present risks or opportunities for investors?

- How does your understanding of sustainability make you a more insightful money manager or financial advisor?

✓ Using courses at your school, build your original thinking on ESG impacts. Construct and track your own simulated portfolio on a website like Google Finance or Motley Fool to test your understanding and application of the concepts

Environmental conservation/nonprofits

Keywords

Environmental conservation, stewardship, nonprofit management, business and environment

Example employers

Conservation International, Environmental Defense Fund, WWF, Natural Resources Defense Council (NRDC), The Conservation Fund, Rare, World Resources Institute, National Park Service, Global Environment & Technology Foundation, US Environmental Protection Agency, The Nature Conservancy, Forest Stewardship Council

Areas of focus

Program management; Administration; Private sector–nonprofit partnerships; Fundraising; Direct marketing

Skills needed

Project management and budgeting; Finance; Business development/fundraising

Key resources

- Environmental Career Center, www.environmental-jobs.com
- Environmental Career Opportunities, www.ecojobs.com
- Green Dream Jobs, www.sustainablebusiness.com/jobs
- World Business Council for Sustainable Development, www.wbcsd.org

Main issues

The environmental conservation movement is not new, of course, but it has not historically been a typical career path for MBAs. In fact, for much of its history, the environmental conservation movement has been in direct opposition to business, and distrustful of business school graduates. For many environmental organizations, that has changed in recent years as they have begun to see opportunities to leverage the resources of the private sector to achieve environmental aims.

Many of the larger environmental conservation nonprofits — or non-governmental organizations (NGOs) — have strategic partnerships with the private sector. Two such examples are Conservation International's Center for Environmental Leadership in Business and Environmental Defense Fund's Corporate Partnerships Program. Other NGO initiatives such as the Natural Resource Defense Council's Center for Market Innovation are developing strategies or policies aimed at market-based solutions to environmental problems. Along with these new partnerships comes an appreciation for the skills that a sustainability-minded MBA student might bring to bear.

There are thousands of environmental organizations working on issues of land, water, air, climate, natural resources, and biodiversity conservation, ranging in scope from local to global. They use a host of different approaches to influence policy, government and corporate action, and consumer behavior to preserve the environment. According to *The Chronicle of Philanthropy*'s 2008 Philanthropy 400,[15] the biggest environmental organizations, based on private charitable contributions raised, are:

- The Nature Conservancy

- WWF

- Trust for Public Land

- Conservation International

- Wildlife Conservation Society

- Natural Resources Defense Council

- Environmental Defense Fund

- The Conservation Fund

- National Wildlife Federation

- National Audubon Society

- Ducks Unlimited

There are also a number of trade and membership organizations working specifically on business and sustainable development issues. These include organizations like:

- Net Impact

- Business for Social Responsibility

- World Business Council for Sustainable Development

- US Business Council for Sustainable Development

- US Green Building Council

- Fair Labor Association

- Ceres

These are not conservation organizations that work with business, but rather business-focused nonprofit associations. Because transforming the private sector is their mission, they often hire MBAs and other professionals who can speak the language of business.

Career search notes

Environmental nonprofit organizations are most likely to hire MBAs for positions in:

- Program management

- Research initiatives related to private-sector partnerships

- Marketing and communications

- Finance

- Development (aka, fundraising)

Governmental agencies like the US Environmental Protection Agency and National Park Service also hire MBAs for internships and full-time positions.

Nonprofit work isn't for every MBA. Some people find NGOs and government agencies to be bureaucratic; others don't like the constant reliance on fundraising. And, of course, there is the salary discrepancy (sometimes more like a chasm) between non-profit salaries and traditional MBA salaries.

But there are pros to nonprofit work as well. For one thing, you have the chance to work with an entire organization of professionals who are equally committed to the cause — which can be inspiring and invigorating. Most nonprofit professionals feel a great deal of satisfaction from working so directly on improving the world for the better. And, despite the salary trade-offs, some nonprofits offer better benefits packages, work–life balance options, and other perks for their employees than private-sector employers.

Example job titles include:

- Program Manager, Industrial Sector, Consortium for Energy Efficiency

- Senior Financial Analyst, Natural Resources Defense Council

- Corporate Partnerships Intern, Environmental Defense Fund

- Real Estate Associate, The Conservation Fund

- Summer Associate, Sustainable Conservation

- Management Analyst, National Park Service

- Intern, Market Research, Rare

Like it or not, many environmental nonprofit professionals are skeptical of MBAs. Some have spent their careers battling big business as activists, and others just don't believe that MBA skills translate to the nonprofit world. One way to overcome this is to demonstrate a serious commitment to the NGO's mission, and add nonprofit experience to your resume as a volunteer or intern. A dual degree (MBA paired with another degree in, for instance, environmental science or forestry) can be another way to stand out. You might also look especially at NGOs that (a) have MBAs on staff already, or (b) have private sector partnership initiatives that go beyond just financial donations.

A note of humility also goes a long way. MBA skills *do* translate to the nonprofit world, but there are also some very unique challenges to working for nonprofits. Unless you have significant nonprofit experience, be cautious of walking into an interview and presuming you know exactly how to "improve" the operation.

Tips

✓ Be sure you believe in, and can demonstrate your personal commitment to, an organization's particular mission. If you're interviewing for a climate change program

After completing her MBA at the University of Virginia's Darden School of Business, Katherine Neebe was committed to working in the field of sustainability, but was open to both for-profit and nonprofit avenues. She worked for a regional sustainability organization and a consultancy before joining WWF in 2007. She is now a senior program officer with WWF where she manages a joint partnership project between WWF and The Coca-Cola Company aimed at conserving freshwater resources around the world, supporting more efficient water use in the company's agricultural supply chain and manufacturing facilities, and reducing the emission of greenhouse gases.

Found her current position . . .

. . . advertised on the Internet, and applied online.

Her job search tips

✓ Revise any preconceived notions about nonprofits. Assume that the people who are interviewing you are intelligent, qualified, and educated

✓ Be persistent and be flexible. This is not an easy field to break into nor is there a defined "track" for an MBA student

✓ Remember that this is still a field relatively new to the MBA community. Informational interviews will advance not only your immediate job priorities, but also your long-term career goals

✓ Send well-written thank-you notes that show attention to detail. Triple-check the correct spelling and wording of the organization's name (e.g., "Federation" is not the same thing as "Fund")

"As part of my job, I've traveled far and wide — from Mozambique to China to Texas — to help draw the linkages between

✓ Remember that most NGOs are mission-driven. Have a compelling story about why you share that focus

environmental concerns and business interests," she says. "Furthermore, to my view, this is a field which is really at the forefront in terms of innovation and it is evolving almost continuously. Each and every day brings new challenges, new developments, and new solutions. This keeps my job and my field fresh and fun to work in." It was a long and winding path to this job for Katherine, so she encourages students not to give up too soon.

When offering advice to students, Katherine stresses the importance of real-world experience. "Nothing makes an MBA candidate more likely to obtain an interview at an NGO or ultimately land a job than real-world experience in the field. This is still a tough arena for someone with an MBA to break into, jobs remain scarce, and there is some degree of a 'pay your dues' mentality." She recommends students design an independent study or practicum opportunity during the academic year, and identify a local or regional NGO to work with on the topic. She adds that students need "a clear sense of the issue or region (ideally both) that they are interested in working in and have a 'story' to tell about it."

Finally, she adds, "The candidates that are successful in their pursuit of full-time employment in this field tend to have a blend of traditional private-sector experience coupled with tangible exposure to sustainability from a NGO (or similar) perspective."

fellowship, but you're spotted driving up to your interview in a gas-guzzling SUV (sport utility vehicle), you may be met with some skepticism

✓ Remember that, first and foremost, nonprofit organizations are mission-driven. While many of the tools of business are useful in the nonprofit world, be careful not to assume that they *all* apply; the organizational drivers, incentives, or success metrics are fundamentally different for nonprofits

✓ Try, if possible, to get a sense of the position's salary range before interviewing. Some NGO positions are simply going to be out of the question from a financial perspective

✓ Get involved with an environmental nonprofit organization in your spare time. Join a board, work on a consulting project, manage a fundraising event, or just volunteer on the weekends. You'll gain contacts and connections, in addition to a strong experience story that you can discuss in interviews

✓ There are thousands of environmental organizations — from global leaders to local community action groups — so finding the right fit can take some time. One place to research organizations is Charity Navigator (www. charitynavigator.org), an independent agency that evaluates nonprofits

✓ There are a host of job posting sites devoted specifically to nonprofit jobs or environmental conservation careers (see list of job posting websites on page 143)

Social entrepreneurship

Keywords

Social entrepreneurship, social return on investment (SROI), nonprofit management, social venture, social enterprise, venture philanthropy, social venture capital

Example employers

Acumen Fund, REDF, Education Pioneers, Echoing Green, The Aspen Institute, College Summit, KIPP, Bill & Melinda Gates Foundation, Greyston Bakery, Focus: HOPE, GlobalGiving, Habitat for Humanity; other nonprofit organizations and social enterprises, nonprofit consulting firms

Areas of focus

Operations/administration; Business planning; Metrics and measurement; Program management

Skills needed

SROI metrics; Project management; Business plan development; Proforma financial analysis; Budgeting

Key resources

- Ashoka, www.ashoka.org
- Bridgestar, www.bridgestar.org
- Changemakers, www.changemakers.net
- Commongood Careers, www.cgcareers.org
- Idealist, www.idealist.org
- Skoll Foundation, www.skollfoundation.org
- Social Edge, www.socialedge.org
- Social Enterprise Alliance, www.se-alliance.org
- Social Venture Network, www.svn.org
- *The Chronicle of Philanthropy*, www.philanthropy.com

Main issues

Like the concept of sustainability itself, social entrepreneurship is another term that means different things depending on who's doing the defining. In general, however, social entrepreneurship is the application of innovative entrepreneurial strategies to solve pressing social problems.

Social entrepreneurship ventures are often nonprofits, but may also be in the private sector, or may be an organizational structure that marries both financial and social goals. Examples of these hybrid organizational types include "B corporations," for-benefit or social-purpose companies, or social enterprises (typically, nonprofit organizations that have revenue-generating or earned-income strategies). For a thoughtful summary of these distinctions, see *The Meaning of "Social Entrepreneurship"* by Professor Greg Dees.[16]

An important topic in the current discussion of social entrepreneurship is metrics and measurement. REDF is one organization that has been pioneering research on the topic of social return on investment (SROI). Other hot topics in the social entrepreneurship space are:

- New and emerging sources of funding (patient capital, social venture capital, venture philanthropy, microfinance)

- The opportunities and challenges of scalability (microfranchising, private–nonprofit partnerships)

The Skoll Foundation, Schwab Foundation, REDF, and Ashoka are some of the most prominent organizations working to advance the practice of social entrepreneurship. They provide funding and other assistance to social entrepreneurs directly, and sponsor studies and fellowships to further the field.

Career search notes

A student interested in social entrepreneurship might choose to work for a social entrepreneur directly — for instance, College Summit, Education Pioneers, OneWorld Health, or KickStart, to name a few. Apart from working directly for an entrepreneurial venture, there are also opportunities to work for one of the organizations that provide services to social entrepreneurs. These include:

- Consultants (e.g., Bridgespan, FSG Social Impact Advisors)

- Funders (e.g., Ashoka, Draper Richards Foundation, REDF)

- Venture philanthropists (e.g., New Profit, Common Good Ventures)

Some students wonder if they should take a traditional MBA position in the corporate world first and return to social entrepreneurship later in their careers. "If students are passionate about social entrepreneurship and have already developed a well-rounded business skill set, I often encourage them to consider pursuing their interests as soon as possible, rather than taking an extended detour through a private-sector career path," says Matt Nash, Managing Director of the Center for the Advancement of Social Entrepreneurship at Duke University's Fuqua School of Business. "The longer you are out there in a career, the harder it is to change." He adds, however, that "this is a very personal decision that must be based upon a student's previous experience as well as their desire for professional development in a private-sector position, income requirements, and ultimate career aspirations."

Example social entrepreneurship jobs posted recently include:

- Project Leader, Urban Challenge, Absolute Return for Kids

- Green Careers Program Director, Global Exchange

- Director of Operations, Every Child Matters Education Fund

- Associate, nonprofit finance fund

- International Business Analyst, MissionFish

- Fellow, Acumen Fund

- Fund Development Coordinator, Institute for OneWorld Health

And, of course, many MBAs interested in social entrepreneurship choose to start their own enterprises. There are a number of business development resources specifically for social entrepreneurship/social enterprise if you choose this route.

When pursing jobs in the field of social entrepreneurship, some students orient themselves based on mission, others based on role. "Some students have a real passion for a particular mission area — for example, education — and then look for a functional role working in that sector. They tend to end up in more program management roles," says Nash. "Other students are more 'mission agnostic.' They tend to be looking for operational roles like CFO or COO. (Though, ultimately, when applying for the job, you still need to demonstrate commitment to the organization's mission, either way.)"

As with other fields covered in this book, real-world experience is the best way to position yourself for a social entrepreneurship career. If you don't have social-sector experience in your pre-MBA career, then you need to find a way to develop that while you are a student (see "Gaining experience" on page 40 for ideas).

Tips

✓ In researching this field, don't miss David Bornstein's excellent book *How to Change the World: Social Entrepreneurs and the Power of New Ideas.*[17] The PBS series, *The New Heroes*, also profiles 12 social entrepreneurs in four episodes

✓ To learn about some of the more accomplished social entrepreneurs and the organizations they've founded, visit the lists of Ashoka Fellows (www.ashoka.org/fellows) and Schwab Foundation social entrepreneurs (www.schwabfound.org), both searchable by country and by sector. Another good starting place is *Fast Company*'s annual Social Capitalist Awards (look at current and past award winners). The Draper Richards Foundation (www.draperrichards.org) and Echoing Green (www.echoinggreen.org) also list fellows on their websites

✓ Consider applying for the highly competitive REDF, Acumen Fund, and Echoing Green annual fellowship programs. There are also a number of innovative foundations that provide resources and funding for sustainable ventures such as the Omidyar Network, the Skoll Foundation, the Schwab Foundation, Draper Richards Foundation, and Mulago Foundation

✓ If you are an aspiring entrepreneur yourself, or would like to team up with one, consider participating in the Global Social Venture Competition — the largest MBA business plan competition devoted specifically to double-bottom-line ventures. Many universities also have business plan competitions that include a social entrepreneurship track

Tim Scheu was fortunate to start his career in social entrepreneurship early. After finishing his undergraduate degree, he happened into an unpaid internship with an organization called Development States — now GlobalGiving — in Washington DC, where he saw the powerful potential of social entrepreneurship. "The longer I spent there, the more I had appreciation for their entrepreneurial spirit," he says.

He decided to return for his MBA at Duke University's Fuqua School of Business to develop the business fundamentals for a career in social entrepreneurship. Tim knew he wanted to focus his post-MBA career on the social sector, but

Found his current position . . .

. . . through personal networking with business school alumni and contacts from his pre-MBA career.

His job search tips

✔ Narrow your focus. Identify a handful of organizations that you are really interested in, and research them. Spend some time understanding the dynamics and the challenges these organizations are facing

✔ Be prepared for a bit of a culture shock, particularly if you're working at a smaller organization. MBAs are sometimes tempted to think that they can walk into an organization and have all the answers. There is a bit of keeping your ego in check needed; understand what you don't know

✔ Recommended reading: I like *Fast Company* and its Social Capitalist Awards. *Stanford Social Innovation Review* is filled with great insights from contemporary non-profit leaders

wasn't sure of the exact path or organization. "There are so many social-sector organizations out there," he says, adding that this can be both an advantage and a disadvantage for job seekers. "Not all of them are a great fit for MBAs, but I never was worried that I wouldn't get a job." On the other hand, he says, after business school, "It's such a blank slate. There can be a paralysis of choice."

Like others, Tim credits networking with his success in his job search. By reaching out to connections in the Fuqua alumni network, and to others he had worked with before business school, Tim developed relationships that led to his eventual job offer.

He now holds the title of Innovation Officer with the organization International Bridges to Justice (IBJ). In his job, he applies the pragmatism and strategic thinking he refined in business school to help IBJ scale its impact and explore the potential of online programming to drive human rights reforms worldwide. "What I love most about this job is flexibility I have to pursue new programs," he says. "Innovation is part of IBJ's DNA and I am happy to contribute to that process."

When talking to students interested in social entrepreneurship, Tim advises them to be patient and persistent. "One of the things you absolutely have to do is demonstrate passion," he says. "The individuals who stand out are ones who can tell a personal story, or demonstrate a commitment to the organization's mission. They have a passion and they follow through on it."

✓ The annual Skoll World Forum on Social Entrepreneurship (www.skollworldforum.com) is the premier conference on this topic. You can view the content live via Internet streaming, and see videos from past conferences online. Other useful events include the conferences of the Clinton Global Initiative, Social Enterprise Alliance, and Investors' Circle

✓ Be prepared for significantly lower salaries in the field of social entrepreneurship. Though salaries for MBAs working in the social sector have been trending upward, these jobs are still likely to pay less than private-sector MBA positions. Competition for these positions is no less intense, however

Green marketing

Keywords

Green marketing, LOHAS, sustainable marketing

Example employers

GreenOrder, J. Ottman Consulting, The Change, Groundswell, Johnson & Johnson, Burt's Bees, Method, Whole Foods, Clif Bar, Timberland, Interface, Honest Tea, Herman Miller, IdealBite, Patagonia, REI; consumer packaged goods companies, natural products companies

Areas of focus

Product and brand management, marketing strategy

Skills needed

Market research, customer and competitor analysis, messaging and communications

Key resources

- Green America's National Green Pages, www.greenamericatoday.org/pubs/greenpages
- *LOHAS Journal* and consumer trend articles, www.lohas.com/journal
- J. Ottman Consulting, www.greenmarketing.com
- Sustainable Life Media, www.sustainablelifemedia.com
- Sustainable Style Foundation, www.sustainablestyle.org

Main issues

Maybe more than any other sustainability discipline, the practice of green marketing is exploding as more and more companies (sincere or otherwise) seek to jump on the green bandwagon.

Green marketing, as the name implies, means marketing and brand management for environmentally friendly products and services. Much of practice is standard marketing (market segmentation, product, price, placement, promotion, etc.), but green marketing may differ at times to include:

- Eco-labeling, green product certification

- Cause marketing in connection with environmental causes

- Distribution through specialty green retailers

- Measuring/communicating a product's life-cycle environmental impacts

- Packaging or production considerations

For instance, it's not enough to develop an environmentally friendly toothpaste; you'll have to think differently about how it's packaged, where it's sold, and how it's promoted.

With so many companies rushing to appeal to green consumers, a major pitfall is "greenwashing" (insincere or unfounded green claims). Companies must do more than ever to demonstrate to consumers that claims are substantiated.

Another important term to know is the "LOHAS" (lifestyles of health and sustainability) consumer segment. This is an important segment that you'll be expected to be well versed in, though it is by no means the only target audience for green products these days.

Career search notes

There are consulting agencies that specialize in green marketing (GreenOrder, J. Ottman Consulting, and others), but the biggest set of opportunities is in working in the in-house marketing department of a green or values-driven company. Obvious examples include companies like Clif Bar, Seventh Generation, Method, Honest Tea, Patagonia, or Burt's Bees, but there are literally thousands of options to market products ranging from fair-trade coffee to organic T-shirts to electric cars.

If you're interested in consumer products, check out the directory of companies in Green America's online "National Green Pages," as well as the lists of products carried at organic grocers like Whole Foods and retailers like Gaiam. You can also get ideas from the advertisers in magazines like *The LOHAS Journal*, *Organic Spa* magazine, *Natural Home*, and *Mother Earth News*, and the attendees and sponsors of relevant conferences like the Natural Products Expos, LOHAS Forum, and Green Festivals.

Diversified consumer or healthcare companies like Procter & Gamble, Johnson & Johnson, Kimberly-Clark, and SC Johnson also have green marketing efforts, and, while consumer products get a lot of attention, there is also plenty of greening in other sectors. Marketing for companies like Toyota, GE, or IBM might all involve some elements of targeted green marketing.

Example green marketing job titles include:

- Manager, New Business Development, Groundswell

- Product Development Manager, Honest Tea

- Product Manager, Hewlett-Packard

- LOHAS Business Director, Natural Marketing Institute

- Senior Brand Manager, Burt's Bees

Coleman Bigelow has always had a passion for environmental issues, but for a long time, it was just an extracurricular pursuit. He spent time volunteering with the Sierra Club and other organizations, but didn't make sustainability the focus of his career.

While at the University of Virginia's Darden School of Business, Coleman pursued a traditional marketing and brand management path. "I was interested in CSR in my extracurricular activities, but I didn't really see a career path in that. It seemed more theoretical, and less like I could make a living in it."

Through on-campus recruiting activities, he found a fit for a brand management

Found his current position . . .

. . . after working for three years as a brand manager and applying for an internal opening.

His job search tips

✓ Look at the product categories where you see green marketing happening and target those companies

✓ Do your due diligence about which companies have authenticity and which are just "greenwashing"

✓ If you end up in a functional role at a traditional/large company, get involved with task forces or committees that reach beyond your department. It is a great way to develop relationships with individuals from other parts of the company

✓ Research, research, research. Start talking to your friends, family, anyone else you know about your passion for this

✓ Greenbiz.com, Joel Makower's blog, and Sustainable Life Media

internship with Pfizer Consumer, and joined the company full-time after graduation. When Pfizer Consumer was acquired by Johnson & Johnson, he continued working on new product launches with Johnson & Johnson.

are good sources of information. Consumer websites like www.Treehugger.com and www.the-dailygreen.com are good ways to keep up with the voice of the consumer

It was part luck, part persistence, and part just being in the right place at the right time that led Coleman to uncover a new position in sustainable brand marketing at Johnson & Johnson. The role offered him the chance to combine his marketing expertise with his environmental interests.

As product manager for sustainable brand marketing, Coleman develops strategies to help translate the value of Johnson & Johnson's environmental stewardship to the marketplace, and drives awareness of sustainability in the marketing community. Part of his job is to build tools and resources that support greener product initiatives, and help Johnson & Johnson marketers develop product positioning for green consumers. "A large part of my role is taking complicated scientific and social issues and translating them in meaningful ways so that internal and external audiences can understand them and take action."

Coleman is glad he began his career in a functional discipline, rather than focusing his job search on sustainability at the outset. "The reason I was hired was because of my marketing background," he says.

"I love the sense of possibility with this job," Coleman says. "We're not only marketing a product that can improve someone's health, but we're also helping to minimize the impact on the environment. And there is a natural connection between the environment and human health." He adds, "I also love the sense of discovery. I feel like I'm learning something new every day."

✓ There are several good conferences to check out related to green marketing. Consider attending the annual "Good and Green" Green Marketing Conference, Sustainable Brands International, Natural Products Expo East or West, LOHAS Forum, and/or Greener by Design

✓ Decide whether you want to work as a brand manager for a values-driven company where you'll be 100% devoted to a green product, or whether you want to work for a large company where you'll get great marketing training but may spend only a fraction of your time on green issues

Additional career paths

Besides those discussed in detail in the previous pages, there are many other possible career paths related to sustainability, some of which are included below. The fields are too numerous and specialized to devote whole pages to these, but they are worth mentioning briefly.

Academia

Universities have been leaders in pushing the sustainability agenda forward, and jobs have followed. Many universities now have full-time sustainability officer positions; some have fully staffed sustainability offices. These positions typically include managing campus sustainability issues like water and energy management, recycling initiatives, transportation impacts, and sustainability measurement/reporting; they may or may not include being involved with sustainability curriculum across campus. An example job title is Director of Sustainability, Rice University.

Another path is managing CSR or sustainable business programs as part of an academic center at a business school or university institute. These positions may involve consulting with companies, writing case studies, or doing research, in addition to program management. An example job title might be Executive Director, Center for Responsible Business at UC–Berkeley's Haas School of Business.

The Association for the Advancement of Sustainability in Higher Education (AASHE) is a great resource for campus sustainability positions. AASHE publishes job descriptions and an annual salary survey of campus sustainability officers on its website (www.aashe.org/resources/sust_professionals.php). It also hosts an annual conference (an excellent networking opportunity) and lists job openings in its weekly e-newsletter.

Social marketing

Different from green marketing, social marketing is the practice of applying marketing tools and techniques to "sell" a socially desirable behavior, rather than a product. Well-known examples are campaigns to reduce smoking or drug use (e.g., the "Truth" or "This is your brain on drugs" ad campaigns), encourage public safety behaviors such as seat belt use, or change environmental awareness or behaviors (e.g., anti-litter campaigns). Social marketing techniques play an important role in public health interventions in many developing countries — for instance, educating communities on proper sanitation practices. (Note: this definition of social marketing is not to be confused with another, emerging use of the term, which refers to marketing through social networking channels like Facebook, LinkedIn, etc.)

Opportunities for social marketing careers exist at consulting firms and agencies (Ogilvy PR, Weinreich Communications), nonprofit organizations (Rare, Population Services International), or at public health agencies like the Centers for Disease Control (CDC). If you're interested in learning more about this field, *Social Marketing Quarterly* (www.socialmarketingquarterly. com) is a great resource to start with.

Cause marketing

Another marketing application is cause marketing. Cause marketing (sometimes also termed "cause-related marketing") is typically a partnership between a company and a nonprofit organization to sell products or services that are linked with a social cause. Campaigns that pledge to give a portion of the proceeds to breast cancer awareness or plant a tree for every product purchased are examples of cause marketing. Ben & Jerry's is well known for its creative cause marketing initiatives (remember

"Peace Pops" and "Rainforest Crunch"). The Product(RED)™ campaign, which supports development organizations in Africa through the sale of branded products from Gap, Apple, Starbucks, and other companies, is another well-known example.

As far as careers go, it is unlikely that cause marketing is a discipline you would be devoted exclusively to unless you were with a consulting firm specializing in the practice (e.g., Cone, Inc., Allison & Partners, MS&L Worldwide). At a consumer products company like Johnson & Johnson or Avon, you might be involved with cause marketing campaigns in the course of other marketing efforts.

The Cause Marketing Forum (www.causemarketingforum.com) is a great place to research this field of practice; see especially the Halo Awards and Case Studies sections for examples of which firms are highly visible in cause marketing.

Cleantech venture capital

Cleantech (sometimes also written "clean tech") venture capital is traditional venture capital invested in environmental and clean energy technologies. Cleantech venture capital (VC) got a big boost after the dot-com bubble burst in 2001. As venture capitalists started moving away from Internet technologies, many saw energy and environmental technologies to be the hot new frontier (Kleiner Perkins is a high-profile example; Al Gore joined the partners in 2007 as the firm shifted its focus). Other example cleantech VCs include EnerTech Capital, Draper Fisher Jurvetson, Chrysalix Energy, and SJF Ventures, to name just a few.

Venture capital, in general, is a difficult field for MBA students to break into right away. Most VCs are looking for more experienced professionals with deep industry expertise. If you are determined to work in VC, networking is crucial. Be sure to attend industry events like those of The Cleantech Group (www.cleantech.com, formerly the Cleantech Venture Network), as well as local clean energy network events. You might be able to work your way in to a cleantech investor forum event (there are many) as a volunteer. Having a rigorous understanding of emerging energy technologies is one way to stand out as an asset in this field; an engineering background and/or pre-MBA experience with energy or environmental technology companies can help.

Social venture capital

Social venture capital differs from traditional or cleantech VC in its fundamental model. Social or sustainable venture capital is an equity investment that seeks to balance financial returns with social or environmental objectives. Social VCs might have a lower hurdle rate or longer time to exit than traditional VCs, but they might also expect specific social outcomes or social returns on their investments.

Social VCs like Good Capital and Acumen Fund are known to hire MBAs for internships and full-time positions immediately after graduation. As with other fields, networking is crucial to finding an entry point in this sector. "Students interested in social venture capital often focus on the financial modeling or business plan analysis aspect of venture capital activities," says Deb Parsons (MBA 2006), Director of Business Development for Investors' Circle. "While these areas are very important, I would not underestimate the other critical piece to being successful in this sector: a diverse network."

Two great resources for researching this field are the Social Venture Network (www.svn.org) and Investors' Circle (www. investorscircle.net). You should also consider participating in the Sustainable Venture Capital Investment Competition (www.svcic.

org), a national MBA competition aimed specifically at understanding the social venture capital evaluation process.

Sustainable banking and finance

Besides socially responsible investing (discussed on pages 85ff.), there are several other ways sustainability intersects with the banking, insurance, and finance industries. These include:

- Issues in products (credit cards, consumer banking products, "green" mortgages)

- Project finance (Equator Principles, Carbon Principles, brownfield investment)

- Lending practices (responsible lending, microfinance)

- Commodities trading (renewable energy credit [REC] trading, carbon trading)

- Community development banking

- Operations

Because there are several points of intersection between sustainability and the finance industry, the jobs are diverse. It is unlikely that you would be dealing with all of the potential sustainability issues in any one position. Typically, you will have to enter the company in a functional role like marketing or trading, and apply your sustainability knowledge in that specific role.

The Environmental Bankers Association (EBA) has a nice, concise summary of these issues in its booklet, *Your Financial Institution and the Environment* (available on its website at www.envirobank.org). EBA also has a Career Center with job postings on its website, as well as a list of related websites. Other useful websites include:

- *The Financial Times' Sustainable Banking Awards* (www. ft.com/sustainablebanking)

- Environmental Finance (www.environmental-finance. com)

- UNEP Finance Initiative (www.unepfi.org)

- Ceres (www.ceres.org)

Community and economic development

Another career path for MBAs interested especially in social issues is community and economic development. Community development organizations work to create jobs, housing, health services, or social programs that serve disadvantaged populations and improve local communities. Career options include roles with:

- Community development financial institutions (CDFIs), which provide credit, investment, and financial services to under-served markets

- Community development corporations (CDCs) that are working to revitalize a community

- Affordable housing real estate developers or lenders

- Small business development organizations that work with minority entrepreneurs or other groups

- Government agencies providing financing and/or business development assistance to disadvantaged communities

- Community development venture capital or investment funds

Community development is not a new field, and there are many opportunities for dedicated, socially oriented MBAs, especially in the realm of finance. Example employers include: ShoreBank, Boston Community Capital, Fannie Mae Corporation, Enterprise, Self-Help Ventures Fund, Mercy Housing, Wachovia Community Development Finance, Corporation for Enterprise Development (CFED), state or local economic development centers, and minority or rural entrepreneurship organizations, to name a few.

There are a host of resources, conferences, and publications devoted specifically to community development finance, economic development, and affordable housing development. Check out organizations like the CDFI Coalition of Community Development Financial Institutions (www.cdfi.org) and the Community Development Venture Capital Alliance (www.cdvca.org) as a start. Use your alumni networks from both your undergraduate and graduate institutions, as you will likely find many alumni working in established community development careers.

International development

Like community development, international development is a vast topic, with many different types of employers and career entry points. Multilateral development agencies like the US Agency for International Development (USAID) are some of the biggest employers; they do hire MBAs, but are more likely to recruit on campus for students with Masters in international policy or international studies than MBAs. Other employers include consultancies that work with the major development agencies (e.g., Development Alternatives Inc., Chemonics) and global non-profit organizations working on development issues (e.g., CARE, Oxfam, Transparency International, CEDPA).

There are numerous websites devoted specifically to international development careers. A few resources to start with include:

- Development Gateway, www.developmentgateway.org

- DevNetJobs, www.devnetjobs.org

- Directory of Development Organizations, www.devdir. org

- World Business Council for Sustainable Development, www.wbcsd.org

The *Vault Guide to International Development Careers*[18] is another good place to start, especially if your school has access to Vault resources through your library or career center. If your business school is part of a university, look across campus for other departments, clubs, and interdisciplinary programs related to international development; your campus might have a global studies center, society for international development, or school of public health that offers terrific opportunities to get involved.

Microfinance

Microfinance is the practice of providing banking services to poor and otherwise unbanked customers in developing countries (or, occasionally, disadvantaged populations in the developed world), and is one of the great development success stories of recent years. Microcredit (or microlending) involves lending very small sums (often $25–200) to poor customers who would otherwise not have access to capital. Microlending institutions often cite repayment rates of higher than 95%, despite requiring no credit history and no collateral from customers.

The field of microfinance gained some much-deserved attention in 2006 when Grameen Bank and its founder, Muhammad Yunus, were awarded the Nobel Peace Prize. Two good books on Grameen and the field of microfinance are Yunus's book *Banker to the Poor: Micro-lending and the Battle against World Poverty*,[19] and David Bornstein's *The Price of a Dream: The Story of the Grameen Bank.*[20]

Besides Grameen, leading microfinance institutions include FINCA International and ACCION International; these organizations do hire MBAs. Some of the larger global banks have experimented with microfinance (e.g., Deutsche Bank's Microcredit Development Fund), and there are also local and regional microfinance organizations working in specific countries. Kiva is another interesting model; with its microfinance partners, Kiva provides a marketplace for individuals anywhere to select and lend directly to entrepreneurs through the Internet.

New microfinance institutions and models are emerging every day. Microfinance Gateway (www.microfinancegateway.org) is a good place to research the field. Two other good resources include:

- Development Gateway's Microfinance Discussion forum (http://microfinance.developmentgateway.org)

- Brigham Young University's *ESR Review* (formerly called the *Journal of Microfinance*)

'Base of the Pyramid' marketing

The term "Base of the Pyramid" (BoP) or "Bottom of the [economic] Pyramid" refers to the roughly four billion people around the world who subsist on less than $2 a day. The term was coined by Professors C.K. Prahalad and Stuart Hart in their 2002 article, "The Fortune at the Bottom of the Pyramid,"[21] in which they propose that serving the world's poor represents not only a responsibility but a market opportunity for multinational corporations. Prahalad's subsequent book *The Fortune at the Bottom of the Pyramid*[22] and Hart's book *Capitalism at the Crossroads*[23] present the case for serving the "BoP" as well as examples from companies like Procter & Gamble, DuPont, and Unilever.

What this means for career paths is harder to define. MBAs passionate about applying BoP strategies may look for opportunities to work on emerging market strategies with a multinational corporation — whether that is from an internal company position (brand or product manager, emerging markets manager), or with a consultancy or nonprofit organization working with companies on this practice (Origo and World Resources Institute are examples).

Next Billion (www.nextbillion.net) is a great resource on this topic and has a Career Center page with job listings. Next Billion also has a nice compilation of recommended reading on the topic.[24]

Final thoughts

There are, of course, additional career options that this guide has not explored in detail in this section. You might be interested in careers in sustainable supply chain management, for instance, or marketing for the ecotourism industry. These are viable career paths for an MBA student. Even though they are not discussed explicitly, many of the career search tips and resources presented in this section still apply.

The next section, Part III, includes additional resources that are helpful in many sustainability job searches, regardless of industry or niche. The MBA job search timeline, recommended reading, news sources and blogs, job boards, and other resources will all help you navigate your sustainability job search.

Timeline and job search resources

This chapter includes the following resources:

- MBA job search timeline
- Key sustainable business Internet resources
- Details of relevant events
- List of recommended reading
- List of job posting websites with sustainability-related opportunities
- Sources of lists of sustainable companies

Appendix A contains a selected list of companies recognized for their sustainability efforts and Appendix B a list of related articles.

MBA job search timeline

MBA first year

August: *Explore*

- Join the national Net Impact organization (www. netimpact.org) and any local school and/or professional chapters

- Read articles and books about sustainability and CSR (see page 141 for "Recommended reading")

- Take a look at the recent sustainability-related job openings posted on related job boards (see page 143 for a list of job posting websites); read the job descriptions and responsibilities associated with different types of positions

- Begin to think about what your particular interests are. Consider:
  - What are your functional interests (finance, marketing, operations, etc.)?
  - What industry interests you?
  - What type of organization interests you most (for-profit, nonprofit, government)?
  - What size organization interests you most (large, small, entrepreneurial)?
  - What (if any) geographic preference do you have?

- Identify upcoming speakers and conferences that you plan to attend for networking opportunities. Register for the Annual Net Impact Conference

- Meet with second-year MBA students to learn about their summer internships in sustainability-related fields

- Make a list of 20–30 organizations that interest you most. Research those organizations, including looking at both their annual reports and their sustainability or corporate citizenship reports. Identify alumni or other contacts at those organizations

- Set up a trip to the geographic region you are targeting (with classmates or on your own) to meet with companies of interest

- Participate in on-campus recruiting activities (i.e., company presentations) for any companies of interest

- Finalize your resume

- Listen in on Net Impact "Issues in Depth" calls on topics of interest (www.netimpact.org)

- Continue reading in your area(s) of interest. Sign up for listservs that will keep you up to date on sustainable business news (e.g., email newsletters from www.greenbiz.com, www.ethicalcorp.com, www.bridgestar.org)

- Conduct informational interviews with alumni, second-years, and practitioners in the field. Ask professors for contacts. Find out if any of your classmates have pre-MBA work experience with your target organizations

- Attend Annual Net Impact Conference (bring resumes for the career expo) and/or other conferences in your area of interest to learn about key industry trends and make contact with industry practitioners (both attendees and presenters)

- Attend events of your local student and professional Net Impact chapters

- Join other local organizations in your field of interest (e.g., Emerging Green Builders, Green Drinks, Sustainable Practice Network) and attend events

- Participate in on-campus recruiting activities

- Stay current on the latest news in your field of interest

- Use class projects as opportunities to delve deeper into subjects of interest and contact relevant industry practitioners. Consider developing a practicum or independent study project to gain project experience in fields of interest

- Write exceptional, personalized cover letters for organizations you are interested in

- Complete at least one mock interview with classmates or second-years to refine your interviewing skills

- Begin internship interviews

- Continue building your network and conducting informational interviews. Follow up with contacts with whom you spoke in the fall

- Check Net Impact job board, and other website job boards

- Send polished, personalized thank you emails to contacts you've met at career events or conducted interviews with (informational or recruiting)

- Prepare for interviews by reading the latest sustainability and CSR news

- Round out your skills through coursework. Take sustainability-related elective courses. Take courses in areas where you are weak on your resume (e.g., marketing or finance) for any skills that might be critical to your internship

- Be patient if openings have not materialized yet; hiring for many sustainability-related roles often happens later in the academic year than for traditional MBA positions. If you have other offers unrelated to your sustainability interests, try to negotiate for more time

- Continue informational interviews and networking

- Check relevant job posting boards and listservs for new openings

- Participate in a sustainability-related case competition, e.g., Net Impact/Leeds Annual Case Competition, Thunderbird's Global Citizenship Challenge, UNC's Sustainable Venture Capital Investment Competition, George Washington University's Nonprofit Case Competition

- Run for a leadership position with your school's Net Impact chapter or other clubs

- Negotiate internship offers

Summer: *Perform*

- Set specific goals at the beginning of your internship: what would you like to accomplish?

- Develop key relationships within the organization and within the sustainability community (investors, consultants, supply chain partners, etc.)

- Network with your classmates, learn what they are doing and meet their co-workers. Contact classmates or professors for help solving strategic challenges or identifying additional resources during the summer

- Remain cognizant of the skills you're utilizing that can be highlighted on your resume

Key sustainable business Internet resources

The table below lists key websites under the headings:

- Resource portals
- Sustainable business news
- Blogs
- Indices and corporate sustainability reports
- Issue briefs and white papers
- Organizations

Resource portals	
GreenBiz	www.greenbiz.com
JustMeans	www.justmeans.com
Sustainable Life Media	www.sustainablelifemedia.com
WiserEarth	www.wiserearth.org
WorldChanging	www.worldchanging.com
Sustainable business news	
Corporate Eco Forum, "CEF Weekly Briefing"	www.corporateecoforum.com
ClimateBiz	www.climatebiz.com
CSRwire	www.csrwire.com
Ecosystem Marketplace	www.ecosystemmarketplace.com
Environmental Finance	www.environmental-finance.com
Environmental Leader	www.environmentalleader.com
Environmental News Network	www.enn.com
Ethical Corporation	www.ethicalcorp.com
GreenBiz	www.greenbiz.com
Next Billion	www.nextbillion.net
SocialFunds.com	www.socialfunds.com
Sustainable Business News	www.sustainablebusiness.com/news/index.cfm

Blogs	
Joel Makower: Two Steps Forward	http://makower.typepad.com
Triple Pundit	www.triplepundit.com
Indices and corporate sustainability reports	
Calvert Social Index	www.calvert.com/sri_calvertindex.html
Ceres Company Sustainability Reports	www.ceres.org/companyreports
Dow Jones Sustainability Indexes	www.sustainability-index.com
Ethibel Sustainability Index	www.ethibel.org/subs_e/4_index/main.html
FTSE4Good Index Series	www.ftse.com/Indices/FTSE4Good_Index_Series
Global 100 Most Sustainable Companies	www.global100.org
Global Reporting Initiative (GRI) corporate reports	www.globalreporting.org
ReportAlert	www.reportalert.info
Issue briefs and white papers	
Business for Social Responsibility (BSR) Issue Briefs	www.bsr.org/research/issue-briefs.cfm
SustainAbility Issue Briefs	www.sustainability.com/insight/issue-briefs.asp
UNC Center for Sustainable Enterprise Knowledge Bank	www.cse.unc.edu/knowledge
Organizations	
Business for Social Responsibility (BSR)	www.bsr.org
Ceres	www.ceres.org
Chicago Climate Exchange	www.chicagoclimatex.com
Pew Center's Business Environmental Leadership Council	www.pewclimate.org/companies_leading_the_way_belc
Social Enterprise Alliance	www.se-alliance.org
Society for Organizational Learning (SoL)	www.solonline.org
US Business Council for Sustainable Development (USBCSD)	www.usbcsd.org
US EPA Climate Leaders	www.epa.gov/stateply
World Business Council for Sustainable Development (WBCSD)	www.wbcsd.org
World Resources Institute	www.wri.org

Relevant events

Below are details of some of the biggest annual sustainability-related conferences. Conferences can be time-consuming and expensive, but they are among the best networking opportunities you'll have because so many industry contacts are assembled in one place. A few conference tips:

- If you want to attend but can't pay the registration fee, email the conference organizers and ask if you can serve as a volunteer (ask several months in advance, if possible). Many conferences will waive the registration fee for volunteers, and, though you may miss some of the panels or plenaries, you usually can still benefit from the networking opportunities

- Review the full list of speakers and panelists at these conferences, whether you can attend or not; you'll get some good ideas about which individuals and companies are influential in the field. Also be sure to pull up the list of conference sponsors and participating companies in the conference "expo," if there is one; these lists will show you which companies are seeking visibility at sustainability events

- Similarly, look at the web pages for past years' conferences. Many of these will post video highlights as well as attendee and speaker lists, all of which is helpful for identifying leads. You'll begin to see patterns in who features regularly

Net Impact national conference

www.netimpact.org

This conference is a "must-attend" for any MBA interested in sustainability careers. Besides being one of the best sustainability conferences around, it features mentoring opportunities, a large career expo, and panels on career development topics specifically for an MBA audience. The event happens annually in the fall, and is usually sold out, so register early.

Business for Social Responsibility (BSR) annual conference

www.bsr.org

Typically held in the fall, this event convenes senior CSR and sustainability executives from some of the most influential companies working on these issues, as well as sustainability consulting firms and nonprofit organizations serving them. Because it is aimed at senior executives, the registration fee to attend is high (over $1,000), but the speakers and networking opportunities are excellent.

Greenbuild international conference and expo

www.greenbuild.org

Greenbuild is the biggest event for anyone interested in the green building industry and its supply chain partners. The 2008 conference drew nearly 30,000 attendees. The conference typically occurs in the fall and offers a substantial discount on registration for students and young professionals.

Sustainable Brands conference
www.sustainablelifemedia.com/events

Sustainable Brands draws about 500 attendees and focuses on the topics of green marketing, consumer attitudes, and brand management. Many of the speakers and attendees are from consumer products companies and retailers. Like BSR, this conference has high registration fees, but students are offered a 30% discount. The conference is typically held in the summer.

Ethical Corporation conferences
www.ethicalcorp.com/conferences

Ethical Corporation convenes several conferences each year on topics including sustainable supply chain management, corporate responsibility reporting, anti-corruption, and an annual responsible business summit. Based in the UK, Ethical Corporation is a good connection for networking with companies from Europe, particularly, but also US and other global leaders.

Bioneers conference
www.bioneers.org

Bioneers draws about 3,000 attendees from academia, industry, and NGOs to discuss leading-edge sustainability topics. The focus is not primarily on business, so much of the program is devoted to topics of ecological design, sustainability science and economics, community activism, and similar issues. Speakers usually include some of the world's most prominent sustainability thought-leaders, and attendees say it is an inspiring event.

Green Festivals

www.greenfestivals.org

Hosted in each year in San Francisco, Washington DC, Seattle and other cities, Green Festivals showcases green goods and services. These events are a great place to learn about local and regional sustainability activities, and network with nonprofits and smaller companies that might not be represented at some of the big-business conferences. Attendance fees are only $10–15.

Investors' Circle conference and Venture Fair

www.investorscircle.net

Investors' Circle hosts two conferences annually, one in the fall and one in the spring. Parts of the conference are only open to members and accredited investors, but the event also includes a day open to a broad audience, featuring speakers on social venture capital topics.

Women's Network for a Sustainable Future (WNSF) annual summit

www.wnsf.org

WNSF hosts an annual summit in New York, and has recently added a West Coast summit. These events are not huge, but the caliber of speakers and the networking opportunities with senior women executives are top-notch.

Co-op America green business conferences

www.coopamerica.org/cabn/conference

Co-op America's conferences, held in Chicago and San Francisco annually, usually engage more values-based private and entrepreneurial companies than those organized by BSR and Ethical Corporation.

Triple Bottom Line Investing (TBLI) conferences

www.tbliconference.com

TBLI hosts two conferences each year — one in Europe and one in Asia — on topics of sustainable finance and socially responsible investing (SRI).

Others

The following websites feature sustainability and CSR-related conference calendars:

- GreenBiz, www.greenbiz.com/resources

- CSRwire, www.csrwire.com/events

- Investors' Circle, www.investorscircle.net/events-1

- Net Impact, http://netimpact.org/calendar.cfm

Recommended reading

Below is a list of some of the most useful titles on sustainability topics for those new to the subject (arranged by publication date, most recent first).

Key sustainable business titles

Winston, A., *Green Recovery: Get Lean, Get Smart, and Emerge from the Downturn on Top* (Harvard Business School Press, 2009).

Schendler, A., *Getting Green Done: Hard Truths from the Front Lines of the Sustainability Revolution* (PublicAffairs, 2009).

Laszlo, C., *Sustainable Value: How the World's Leading Companies Are Doing Well by Doing Good* (Greenleaf Publishing, 2008).

Makower, J., *Strategies for the Green Economy: Opportunities and Challenges in the New World of Business* (McGraw-Hill, 2008).

Hart, S.L., *Capitalism at the Crossroads: Aligning Business, Earth, and Humanity* (Wharton School Publishing, 2nd edn, 2007).

Esty, D.C., and A.S. Winston, *Green to Gold: How Smart Companies Use Environmental Strategy to Innovate, Create Value, and Build Competitive Advantage* (Yale University Press, 2006).

Savitz, A.W., and K. Weber, *The Triple Bottom Line: How Today's Best-Run Companies Are Achieving Economic, Social and Environmental Success — and How You Can Too* (Jossey-Bass, 2006).

Prahalad, C.K., *The Fortune at the Bottom of the Pyramid: Eradicating Poverty through Profits* (Wharton School Publishing, 2005).

Gunther, M., *Faith and Fortune: The Quiet Revolution to Reform American Business* (Crown Business, 2004).

Bornstein, D., *How to Change the World: Social Entrepreneurs and the Power of New Ideas* (Oxford University Press, 2004).

Laszlo, C., *The Sustainable Company: How to Create Lasting Value through Social and Environmental Performance* (Island Press, 2003).

Holliday, C.O., S. Schmidheiny, and P. Watts, *Walking the Talk: The Business Case for Sustainable Development* (Greenleaf Publishing, 2002).

McDonough, W., and M. Braungart, *Cradle to Cradle: Remaking the Way We Make Things* (North Point Press, 2002).

Hawken, P., A.L. Lovins, and H. Lovins, *Natural Capitalism: Creating the Next Industrial Revolution* (Little, Brown and Co., 1999; www.natcap.org/sitepages/pid5.php, July 2009).

Benyus, J.M., *Biomimicry: Innovation Inspired by Nature* (HarperCollins, 1997).

Hawken, P., *The Ecology of Commerce: A Declaration of Sustainability* (Harper Business, 1993).

Career-related titles

Albion, M., *More Than Money: Questions Every MBA Needs to Answer: Redefining Risk and Reward for a Life of Purpose* (BK Life, 2008).

Marquardt, F., *Green Careers: Wetfeet Insiders Guide* (Wetfeet.Com, 2008).

Net Impact, *Social Impact Career Handbook* (Net Impact, 2008; available to members from the Net Impact website [www.netimpact.org]).

Everett, M., *Making a Living While Making a Difference: Conscious Careers for an Era of Interdependence* (New Society Publishers, 2007).

Dorsey, C.L., and L. Galinsky, *Be Bold: Create a Career with Impact* (Echoing Green, 2006).

Albion, M., *Making a Life, Making a Living: Reclaiming Your Purpose and Passion in Business and in Life* (Grand Central Publishing, 2000).

Job posting websites

The websites listed in the table below post sustainability-related jobs and internship opportunities. Sites highlighted in bold tend to be the best sustainability job listings to start with.

Organization	Website	General sustainability	CSR	Environmental	International development	Energy	Non-profit	Other
American Wind Energy Association — Job Board	www.awea.org/employment					X		
Association for the Advancement of Sustainability in Higher Education — Weekly Bulletin, Jobs & Internships Section	www.aashe.org/publications/bulletin.php							X
Boston College Center for Corporate Citizenship — Career Center	**www.bcccc.net/index.cfm?pageId= 2020**	X	X					
Business for Social Responsibility (BSR) — CSR Jobs Board	**www.bsr.org/resources/jobs**	X	X					
Care2 Job Finder	http://jobs.care2.com/a/all-jobs/list			X		X	X	
Chronicle of Philanthropy — Philanthropy Careers Center	http://philanthropy.com/jobs						X	
Corporate Citizenship Briefing — CSR Jobs Board	www.ccbriefing.co.uk/ccb/csr_jobs	X	X					
Council on Foundations — Career Center	www.cof.org/Jobs						X	
CSR Europe	www.csreurope.org/jobs		X					

Organization	Website	General sustainability	CSR	Environmental	International development	Energy	Non-profit	Other
CSR Jobs Yahoo! Group	http://finance.groups.yahoo.com/group/csr-jobs	x	x					
Development Executive Group — Job Postings	www.devex.com/jobs			x		x		
DevNetJobs	www.devnetjobs.org			x	x		x	
Dev-zone Development Jobs (Pacific)	www.dev-zone.org/jobs				x			
EcoEmploy	www.ecoemploy.com			x	x			
Environment Jobs UK	www.environmentjob.co.uk	x		x				
Environmental Career Center	www.environmentalcareer.com			x	x			
Environmental Career Opportunities	www.ecojobs.com			x		x		
Ethical Performance — CSR & SRI Job Board	**www.ethicalperformance.com/recruitment/index.php**	**x**	**x**					
European Sustainable Investment Forum — SRI Job Board	www.eurosif.org/sri/jobs	x						x
ExecSearches Nonprofit Job Board	www.execsearches.com						x	
Foreign Policy Association — Job Board	www.fpa.org/jobs_contact2423/jobs_contact.htm				x			
Foundation Center — Nonprofit Jobs	http://fdncenter.org/pnd/jobs						x	
Green Career Central	www.greencareercentral.com			x		x		
Green Dream Jobs	**www.sustainablebusiness.com/jobs**	**x**		**x**				
Green Jobs	www.greenjobs.com					x		
GreenBiz — JobLink	www.greenbiz.com/jobs/viewjobs.cfm	x		x			x	
Idealist	www.idealist.org				x		x	
International Association of Business Communicators (public/community affairs)	http://jobs.iabc.com		x					X

Organization	Website	General sustainability	CSR	Environmental	International development	Energy	Non-profit	Other
JustMeans	**www.justmeans.com/jobsearch**	x	x				x	x	
Lifeworth	www.lifeworth.com	x	x						
MBAs without Borders — Job Openings	http://projects.mbaswithoutborders.org				x		X	
National Association of Development Organizations	www.nado.org/jobops/index.php						x	x
Net Impact — Career Center	**www.netimpact.org/career**	x	x				x	
Nonprofit Careers Job Bank	www.nonprofitcareer.com						x	
NonProfitOyster	www.nonprofitoyster.com						x	
Oneworld.net jobs	www.oneworld.net/jobs	x		x	x			
Opportunities in Public Affairs	www.brubach.com							X
Opportunity Knocks	www.opportunitynocs.org						x	
REDF Fellows program	www.redf.org/careers-intro.htm						x	
ReliefWeb	www.reliefweb.int/vacancies				x			
Renewable Energy World — Jobs Board	www.renewableenergyworld.com/rea/jobs					x		
Reuters AlertNet	www.alertnet.org/thepeople/jobs				x			
Social Investment Forum — Socially Responsible Investing Job Board	www.svn.org/jobs	x						X
Social Venture Network — Job Listings	www.svn.org/index.cfm?pageId=795	x					x	
SustainabilityForum.com — jobs & internships folder	www.sustainabilityforum.com/forum/job-offers-internships	x	x	x				
The Environmental Organization Web Directory	www.webdirectory.com/Employment			x				

Organization	Website	General sustainability	CSR	Environmental	International development	Energy	Non-profit	Other
WiserEarth, Jobs Page	www.wiserearth.org/job	X	X	X			X	
Recruitment agencies								
Acre	www.acre-resources.co.uk	X	X	X				
Allen & York	www.allen-york.com			X		X		
Bridgestar — Nonprofit Job Board	www.bridgestar.org						X	
Bright Green Talent	www.brightgreentalent.com	X				X		
Careers in Nonprofits	www.careersinnonprofits.com						X	
Dibari & Associates	www.dibari.net	X						
Ellen Weinreb Sustainability Recruiting	www.ellenweinreb.com	X	X					
Energy into Energy	www.energyintoenergy.com					X		
Isaacson, Miller	www.imsearch.com			X			X	X
IvyExec	www.ivyexec.com					X		
Martha Montag Brown & Associates	www.marthamontagbrown.com/searches.html	X	X					
Career coaching								
Ande Diaz Educational Consulting	www.andediazconsulting.com						X	X
Bright Green Talent	www.brightgreentalent.com/jobseekers/coaching	X				X		
Barbara Parks, Green Career Tracks	www.greencare146ertracks.com	X		X				

Note: all sites were accessible as of August 2009

Disclaimer: this list is not intended to be exhaustive; inclusion in the list does not constitute an endorsement

Sustainable companies

A number of sources of lists of companies related to social and environmental sustainability issues are given in the table below. These lists can be an excellent way to start researching companies that are active on sustainability and CSR issues.

Keep in mind that some of these lists are rankings that are selective or exclusionary, while others are organizations where membership is voluntary. The sustainability indices are investment indices so will, by definition, be comprised of publicly traded companies that are then evaluated or screened based on social and environmental criteria. Most mission-driven organizations will not appear on these indices because they are privately held or employee-owned, or social enterprises. The membership lists of organizations/networks below (and other similar groups) are one way to identify some of these mission-driven organizations that will not appear on the indices or rankings.

In Appendix A, I have compiled my own list of some of the large, public companies that have received recognition for sustainability efforts.

Sustainability indices	
Calvert Social Index	www.calvert.com/sri_calvertindex.html
Domini 400 Social Index	www.kld.com/indexes/ds400index
Dow Jones Sustainability Indexes	www.sustainability-index.com
Ethibel Sustainability Index	www.ethibel.org/subs_e/4_index/main.html
FTSE4Good Index	www.ftse.com/Indices/FTSE4Good_Index_Series
FTSE KLD Global Sustainability Index	www.kld.com/indexes/gsindex
Rankings	
CRO's "100 Best Corporate Citizens"	www.thecro.com
Fast Company's "Social Capitalist Awards"	www.fastcompany.com/social
Fortune's "100 Best Companies to Work For"	http://money.cnn.com/magazines/fortune/bestcompanies

Fortune's "Most 'Accountable' Companies"	http://money.cnn.com/magazines/fortune/global500/2007/accountability/full_list.html
Fortune's "World's Most Admired Companies"	http://money.cnn.com/magazines/fortune/mostadmired
Global 100 Most Sustainable Corporations	www.global100.org

Membership organizations/networks

1% for the Planet members	www.onepercentfortheplanet.org
B Corporations (for-benefit companies)	www.bcorporation.net/community
Business for Innovative Climate & Energy Policy (BICEP)	www.ceres.org/bicep
Business for Social Responsibility (BSR) members	www.bsr.org
Ceres members	www.ceres.org
Chicago Climate Exchange members	www.chicagoclimatex.com
EPA Climate partners	www.epa.gov/stateply/partners
Fair Trade Federation members	www.fairtradefederation.com
Global Reporting Initiative participants	www.globalreporting.org/GRIReports/GRIReportsList
Green America's Green Business Network	www.greenamericatoday.org/cabn
US Climate Action Partnership members	www.us-cap.org/about/members/index.asp
WBCSD members	www.wbcsd.org

Appendix A
Select list of companies

For students interested in corporate sustainability, the following list gives you a selection of some of the large, publicly traded corporations that have been active recently on sustainability indices, rankings, and associations. This does not include all of the companies that appear on all of these indices; it is merely a snapshot of some of the more visible ones.

Key:

100 Best Corporate Citizens (2008) = 100 Best Corporate Citizens, 2008, *The CRO* magazine, www.thecro.com/node/615

Calvert Social Index = listed on the Calvert Social Index® (as of January 2009), www.calvertgroup.com/sri-index.html

DJSI US = listed on Dow Jones Sustainability Indexes, DJSI US Index (as of January 2009), www.sustainability-index.com

DJSI World (2009) = listed on Dow Jones Sustainability Indexes, DJSI World Index (as of January 2009), www.sustainability-index.com

Fortune's Most Accountable (2007) = *Fortune* magazine accountability ranking, 2007; http://money.cnn.com/magazines/fortune/global500/2007/accountability/full_list.html

Global 100 (2009) = "Global 100 Most Sustainable Corporations in the World", 2009 list, www.global100.org

Member, BSR = member of Business for Social Responsibility (as of January 2009), www.bsr.org

Member, WBCSD = member of the World Business Council for Sustainable Development (as of January 2009), www.wbcsd.org

Partner, EPA Climate Leaders = Partner or Charter Partner in the US Environmental Protection Agency's Climate Leaders Program (as of April 2009), www.epa.gov/stateply/partners/index.html

Company	Country	Sector	Global 100 (2009)	100 Best Corporate Citizens (2008)	DJSI World (2009)	Other
3M	USA	Industrials			x	Member, WBCSD; Calvert Social Index; DJSI USA; Partner, EPA Climate Leaders
Acciona	Spain	Utilities	x		x	Member, WBCSD
Adidas	Germany	Consumer discretionary	x		x	Member, WBCSD; Member, BSR
Advanced Micro Devices	USA	Information technology	x		x	Calvert Social Index; DJSI USA; Charter Partner, EPA Climate Leaders
Alcoa	USA	Materials	x			Member, WBCSD; DJSI USA; Charter Partner, EPA Climate Leaders
Bank of America	USA	Financials		x	x	*Fortune*'s Most Accountable (2007); Calvert Social Index; Partner, EPA Climate Leaders
BASF	Germany	Materials	x		x	Member, WBCSD; *Fortune*'s Most Accountable (2007)
Baxter International	USA	Healthcare	x	x	x	DJSI USA; Member, BSR; Charter Partner, EPA Climate Leaders
BG Group	UK	Energy	x		x	Member, WBCSD; Member, BSR
BHP Billiton	Australia	Materials	x		x	Member, WBCSD
BP	UK	Energy			x	Member, WBCSD; *Fortune*'s Most Accountable (2007); Member, BSR
Caterpillar	US	Industrials			x	Member, WBCSD; DJSI USA; Member, BSR; Partner, EPA Climate Leaders
Cisco Systems	USA	Information technology		x	x	Calvert Social Index; DJSI USA; Member, BSR; Partner, EPA Climate Leaders
Citigroup	USA	Financials		x	x	*Fortune*'s Most Accountable (2007); Calvert Social Index; DJSI USA; Member, BSR; Partner, EPA Climate Leaders

Company	Country	Sector	Global 100 (2009)	100 Best Corporate Citizens (2008)	DJSI World (2009)	Other
Coca-Cola Company	USA	Consumer staples	x	x		Member, WBCSD; DJSI USA; Member, BSR; Partner, EPA Climate Leaders
Credit Agricole	France	Financials	x			*Fortune's* Most Accountable (2007)
Cummins	USA	Industrials		x	x	Calvert Social Index; DJSI USA; Partner, EPA Climate Leaders
Deere & Co.	USA	Industrials		x		Calvert Social Index; Partner, EPA Climate Leaders
Dell	USA	Informa- tion tech- nology	x		x	Calvert Social Index; DJSI USA; Member, BSR; Partner, EPA Climate Leaders
Dow Chemical	USA	Materials		x	x	Member, WBCSD; DJSI USA; Partner, EPA Climate Leaders
DuPont	USA	Materials				Member, WBCSD; DJSI USA; Partner, EPA Climate Leaders
Eastman Kodak	USA	Consumer dis- cretionary	x			Calvert Social Index; DJSI USA; Charter Partner, EPA Climate Leaders
Eni SpA	Italy	Energy			x	Member, WBCSD; *Fortune's* Most Accountable (2007); Member, BSR
Entergy	USA	Utilities		x	x	Member, WBCSD; DJSI USA; Partner, EPA Climate Leaders
Exelon	USA	Utilities		x		Member, WBCSD; DJSI USA; Partner, EPA Climate Leaders
FPL Group	USA	Utilities	x	x		Charter Partner, EPA Climate Leaders
Gap	USA	Consumer dis- cretionary		x		Calvert Social Index; DJSI USA; Member, BSR; Partner, EPA Climate Leaders
General Electric	USA	Industrials		x	x	Member, WBCSD; *Fortune's* Most Accountable (2007); DJSI USA; Member, BSR; Partner, EPA Climate Leaders
Genzyme Corp.	USA	Healthcare	x			Calvert Social Index; DJSI USA; Partner, EPA Climate Leaders

Company	Country	Sector	Global 100 (2009)	100 Best Corporate Citizens (2008)	DJSI World (2009)	Other
GlaxoSmithKline	UK	Healthcare	x		x	Member, BSR
Goldman Sachs Group	USA	Financials	x	x		*Fortune*'s Most Accountable (2007); Calvert Social Index; DJSI USA; Member, BSR
Hewlett-Packard	USA	Information technology	x		x	*Fortune*'s Most Accountable (2007); Calvert Social Index; DJSI USA; Member, BSR
Honda Motor Co.	Japan	Consumer discretionary	x			Member, WBCSD; *Fortune*'s Most Accountable (2007)
IBM	USA	Information technology		x	x	Member, WBCSD; *Fortune*'s Most Accountable (2007); Calvert Social Index; DJSI USA; Member, BSR; Charter Partner, EPA Climate Leaders
Intel	USA	Information technology	x	x	x	Calvert Social Index; DJSI USA; Member, BSR; Partner, EPA Climate Leaders
ITT Corp.	USA	Industrials		x	x	Member, WBCSD
Kraft Foods	USA	Consumer staples		x	x	DJSI USA; Member, BSR
MeadWestvaco	USA	Materials		x	x	Member, WBCSD; Calvert Social Index; DJSI USA
Motorola	USA	Information technology		x	x	Calvert Social Index; DJSI USA
Munich Re	Germany	Financials	x		x	*Fortune*'s Most Accountable (2007)
Nike	USA	Consumer discretionary	x	x	x	Calvert Social Index; DJSI USA; Member, BSR
Nokia	Finland	Information technology	x		x	Member, WBCSD
Novo Nordisk	Denmark	Healthcare	x		x	Member, WBCSD; Member, BSR
Novozymes	Denmark	Materials	x		x	Member, WBCSD

Company	Country	Sector	Global 100 (2009)	100 Best Corporate Citizens (2008)	DJSI World (2009)	Other
Office Depot	USA	Consumer dis-cretionary		x	x	Calvert Social Index; DJSI USA; Partner, EPA Climate Leaders
PepsiCo	USA	Consumer staples		x	x	Member, WBCSD; Calvert Social Index; DJSI USA; Partner, EPA Climate Leaders
PG&E	USA	Utilities	x	x		DJSI USA
Procter & Gamble	USA	Consumer staples	x			Member, WBCSD; *Fortune's* Most Accountable (2007); Calvert Social Index; DJSI USA; Member, BSR
Prudential	UK	Financials	x			*Fortune's* Most Accountable (2007); Calvert Social Index
Roche Holdings Limited	Switzer-land	Healthcare	x		x	Partner, EPA Climate Leaders
Royal Dutch Shell	Nether-lands	Energy			x	Member, WBCSD; *Fortune's* Most Accountable (2007)
SAP	Germany	Informa-tion tech-nology	x		x	Member, BSR
Sompo Japan Insurance	Japan	Financials	x		x	Member, WBCSD
Staples	USA	Consumer dis-cretionary		x	x	Calvert Social Index; DJSI USA; Charter Partner, EPA Climate Leaders
Starbucks	USA	Consumer dis-cretionary		x	x	Calvert Social Index; DJSI USA; Member, BSR
State Street Corp.	USA	Financials	x	x	x	Calvert Social Index; DJSI USA; Member, BSR
Statoilhydro	Norway	Energy	x		x	Member, WBCSD; *Fortune's* Most Accountable (2007)
Stora Enso	Finland	Materials	x			Member, WBCSD; Partner, EPA Climate Leaders
Sun Microsystems	USA	Informa-tion tech-nology		x		Calvert Social Index; Partner, EPA Climate Leaders

Company	Country	Sector	Global 100 (2009)	100 Best Corporate Citizens (2008)	DJSI World (2009)	Other
Target Corp.	USA	Consumer discretionary		x		*Fortune*'s Most Accountable (2007); Calvert Social Index; DJSI USA; Charter Partner, EPA Climate Leaders
TNT NV	Netherlands	Industrials	x		x	Member, WBCSD
Total	France	Energy			x	*Fortune*'s Most Accountable (2007); Calvert Social Index; Member, BSR
Toyota Motor Corp.	Japan	Consumer discretionary	x		x	Member, WBCSD; *Fortune*'s Most Accountable (2007); Member, BSR
Unilever	UK	Consumer staples	x		x	Member, WBCSD; Member, BSR; Charter Partner, EPA Climate Leaders
United Technologies Corp.	USA	Industrials	x		x	Member, WBCSD; DJSI USA; Member, BSR; Partner, EPA Climate Leaders
Vestas Windsystems	Denmark	Industrials	x			Member, WBCSD
Vodafone Group	UK	Telecommunication services			x	Member, WBCSD; *Fortune*'s Most Accountable (2007)
Wal-Mart Stores	USA	Consumer staples				*Fortune*'s Most Accountable (2007); Member, BSR
Walt Disney	USA	Consumer discretionary	x	x	x	DJSI USA; Member, BSR
Weyerhaeuser	USA	Materials		x		Member, WBCSD; Calvert Social Index; DJSI USA

Appendix B
Related articles

"Carbon job market booming but talent pool is dry," *Reuters*, November 14, 2007.

"Good, Green Jobs: A No-Nonsense Guide to Environmental Jobs and Careers," www.greenbiz.com, October 2005.

Alsop, R., 'Recruiters Seek MBAs Trained in Responsibility,' *Wall Street Journal Online*, December 13, 2005.

Doyle, K., "Remake a Living: Growing the Green Economy," www.grist.org, April 9, 2007.

Eaton, S., "Getting a Slice of the Green Economy," American Public Media, Marketplace Radio, April 13, 2007.

Fister Gale, S., "How to Climb (or Get On) the Green Corporate Ladder," www.greenbiz.com, March 30, 2009.

Guevarra, L., "Jumping into the Green Job Market," www.greenbiz.com, March 30, 2009.

Kamenetz, A., "Ten Best Green Jobs for the Next Decade," *Fast Company*, January 13, 2009.

Mattioli, D., "More Employers Are Going Green," *Wall Street Journal Online*, November 14, 2007.

Schendler, A., "How Do I Find a Green Job?" Aspen Skiing Company; www.aspensnowmass.com/environment/aboutEAC/greenjobs.cfm, July 2009.

Wingfield, B., "Special Report: Going Green. For Job Market, Green Means Growth," www.forbes.com, July 3, 2007.

Endnotes

1 "KPMG International Survey of Corporate Responsibility Reporting" (KPMG International, 2008).
2 David B. Montgomery and Catherine A. Ramus, "Calibrating MBA Job Preferences," working paper, 2008.
3 World Commission on Environment and Development, *Our Common Future* (Oxford University Press, 1987): Chapter 2: Towards Sustainable Development.
4 P. Hawken, A.L. Lovins, and H. Lovins, *Natural Capitalism: The Next Industrial Revolution* (Little, Brown and Co., 1999; www.natcap.org/sitepages/pid5.php, July 2009).
5 "2006 Profile of the Profession" (Boston College Center for Corporate Citizenship, 2006).
6 T.M. Jones, "Corporate Social Responsibility Revisited, Redefined," *California Management Review* 22.3 (1980): 9-67.
7 "The McKinsey Global Survey of Business Executives: Business and Society" (McKinsey & Company, 2006).
8 "KPMG International Survey on Corporate Responsibility Reporting."
9 "The 2006 Cone Millennial Cause Study" (Cone Inc., 2006).
10 Hawken, *et al.*, *op. cit.*
11 For a nice summary, see G.H. Kats, *Green Building Costs and Financial Benefits* (Massachusetts Technology Collaborative, 2003; www.cap-e.com/ewebeditpro/items/O59F3481.pdf, July 2009).
12 P. Roberts, *The End of Oil: On the Edge of a Perilous New World* (Houghton Mifflin Harcourt, 2004); D. Yergin, *The Prize: The Epic Quest for Oil, Money and Power* (Simon & Schuster, 1991); J. Rikfin, *The Hydrogen Economy: The Creation of the Worldwide Energy Web and the Redistribution of Power On Earth* (J.P. Tarcher, 2002); K.S. Deffeyes, *Hubbert's Peak: The Impending World Oil Shortage* (Princeton University Press, 2001).

13 See www.socialinvest.org/resources/research.

14 *Responsible Investing: A Paradigm Shift. From Niche to Mainstream* (Robeco and Booz & Company, 2008).

15 http://philanthropy.com/stats/philanthropy400

16 J.G. Dees, *The Meaning of "Social Entrepreneurship"* (revised 2001; www.caseatduke.org/documents/dees_sedef.pdf, July 2009).

17 D. Bornstein, *How to Change the World: Social Entrepreneurs and the Power of New Ideas* (Oxford University Press, 2004).

18 *Vault Guide to International Development Careers* (Vault Inc., 2008).

19 M. Yunus, *Banker to the Poor: Micro-lending and the Battle against World Poverty* (PublicAffairs, 1999).

20 D. Bornstein, *The Price of a Dream: The Story of the Grameen Bank* (University of Chicago Press, 1997).

21 C.K. Prahalad and S.L. Hart, "The Fortune at the Bottom of the Pyramid," *strategy + business* 16 (1Q2002); www.cs.berkeley.edu/~brewer/ict4b/Fortune-BoP.pdf, July 2009.

22 C.K. Prahalad, *The Fortune at the Bottom of the Pyramid* (Wharton School Publishing, 2005).

23 S.L. Hart, *Capitalism at the Crossroads: The Unlimited Business Opportunities in Solving the World's Most Difficult Problems* (Wharton School Publishing, 2005).

24 G. Augustine, "BoP 101: A Review of 'Must-Read' Literature for Those Interested in the Base of the Pyramid," *Next Billion*, October 1, 2008; www.nextbillion.net/blog/2008/10/01/bop-101-a-review-of-must-read-literature-for-those-interested-i2, July 2009.

Index